Growing Medical Marijuana

Cannabineae.

Cannabis sativa L.

W. Müller.

Growing Medical Marijuana

Securely and Legally

Dave DeWitt

TEN SPEED PRESS
Berkeley

Library of Congress Cataloging-in-Publication Data

    DeWitt, Dave.
    Growing medical marijuana : securely and legally / Dave DeWitt.—1st ed.
      p. cm.
    Includes bibliographical references and index.
    1. Cannabis. 2. Marijuana—Therapeutic use. 3. Cooking (Marijuana) I. Title.
    SB295.C35D49 2013
    615.7'827—dc23
             2012026477

ISBN 978-1-60774-428-3
eISBN 978-1-60774-429-0

Printed in China
Design by Sarah Pulver

10 9 8 7 6 5 4 3 2 1

First Edition

Contents

Introduction

Meet Leo, Novice Marijuana Grower, Age 70

This book is a growing guide designed for beginning to moderately experienced gardeners who, for medical reasons, wish to incorporate this controversial plant into their planned or existing gardening operations. It is not a guide for the mass production of marijuana for profit, nor a stoner's guide, nor a technical treatise of advanced techniques and hundreds of varieties. Rather, it's for people like me who love experimental cultivation and the challenge of growing something new and different.

My parents were avid gardeners in the 1950s, with my mother entering her tulips in flower shows and my father a dedicated tomato grower. My brother Rick and I were the grunts, the ones who turned the compost and mixed the potting soil according to Dad's formula of aged compost, peat moss, sand, and topsoil. But we really learned how to grow things, and soon developed a gardening obsession that we both celebrate ritually every year.

Now I'm known as the "Pope of Peppers," partially due to the fact that I've coauthored three gardening books specifically on chile peppers, and dozens of other books about cooking with them. But before the hot stuff, I grew marijuana clandestinely, off and on, for twenty years, starting forty years ago. I no longer cultivate it because I do not have state certification to do so and my property is not secure enough. Therefore, I'd like to introduce my collaborator, Leo Lascaux, who is the medical marijuana grower featured in this book. Leo is a longtime, close friend of mine, and he's agreed to consult with me on this project with one condition: anonymity. So I won't tell you his real name or where he lives, but he does reside in a state where growing marijuana is legal with state certification, which he has. Throughout this book, I'll chronicle his experiences as a first-time marijuana grower so you can learn from his successes and his mistakes, and I'll show you plenty of photographs of what Leo calls his "marijuana oasis." Before he started growing marijuana, Leo was not a gardener. But he is now. He finally found the right crop.

Leo Lascaux, incognito

Legal vs. Illegal Growing

This gardening guide assumes that you will be growing where it is legal to do so by state law. People can cultivate in fourteen of the seventeen states where it is legal to possess marijuana (at this writing): Alaska, Arizona, California, Colorado, Connecticut, Hawaii, Maine, Michigan, Montana, Nevada, New Mexico, Oregon, Rhode Island, Vermont, and Washington. Home cultivation is not allowed in Delaware, New Jersey, or the District of Columbia, and a special license is required in

New Mexico. In Arizona, patients can only cultivate if they lived twenty-five miles or more from a dispensary when they applied for their card. The various state laws and regulations change frequently, so you should stay informed by consulting the website of the National Organization for the Reform of Marijuana Laws (NORML) at norml.org. Remember that the amount of marijuana that you may possess or cultivate differs from state to state, so please check your state and local ordinances.

It doesn't matter to me whether you're growing marijuana to get high or get cured, or both. It's my job to guide you as a gardener and help you produce the best possible legal crop, given the constantly changing policies about growing and using marijuana, while taking into consideration the remarkable advances in marijuana cultivation since I first grew it forty years ago. Feminized seed, miniature and autoflowering varieties, superior cloning techniques, and other improvements in growing methods now greatly enhance the marijuana gardening experience. It is my hope that gardeners can seamlessly introduce marijuana into their existing gardens and simply enjoy it as another plant that is beneficial to humankind. And remember, chile plants were once simply tolerated weeds that eventually became valuable crops. The same thing is happening to marijuana, and it's about time!

Here are a few questions to ask yourself before planning your medical marijuana garden. What are your motivations and goals? Are you sure you're growing legally? Do you have a secure location for the garden? Are

you going to brag about it to your friends or sell part of the harvest to them? Your motivations and goals must be balanced against the possible consequences of the project you're about to undertake. First, there is a relatively high cost of setup for an indoor growing operation that needs lighting, ventilation, sometimes reflectors, and other equipment. Second is the risk factor. With some states liberalizing their laws about this common weed that was first just tolerated and now quite celebrated, there's a tendency to be lured into a false sense of security. To you and your friends, who may have indulged for years, growing marijuana is commonplace and the feeling that "everyone does it" is pervasive.

Resist that attitude and remember that the majority of people in this country still believe that marijuana, like liquor during Prohibition, is evil and should be banned. Also remember that marijuana is still illegal at the federal level, despite the laws of certain enlightened states, and that flaunting what you are doing is not wise, especially if you are selling part of your crop rather than merely growing it for your own use as medical marijuana. If, for example, someone turns you in to the Drug Enforcement Administration (DEA) for, say, interstate trafficking, your house and all your property could be seized. And you also would have a new, severely downsized place of residence without a garden.

Growing marijuana can be challenging because it is such a valuable crop, even in small quantities. Thieves are unlikely to infiltrate your property to steal tomatoes, but with a single marijuana plant worth upward of a thousand dollars retail, the scenario changes radically. I recommend taking exactly the same precautions that you would take to grow marijuana illegally because, despite the fact that you may be growing legally, if you're not careful, marijuana is as easy to steal from an unsecured location as my cacti collection was from my front patio. That happened because I forgot to lock the gate, and someone backed a truck into my driveway and stole all the large specimens that I had collected for years. Renegade landscapers, perhaps? This is why security is one of the first chapters in this book. So before you plant the first seed, ask yourself if it's worth it to risk your time, money, and

possibly your household security to grow a few highly valuable plants. If you think it *is* worth it, then it's time to start planning. To help you with your planning, let's begin by looking at the organization of this growing guide.

Because I'm tracking the successes and problems of a novice grower, I've organized this guide in a roughly chronological order that follows a typical growing season. The season is arranged in the following stages: fundamentals and planning (chapters 1–4), growing (chapters 5–7), harvesting and storage (chapter 8), problems (chapter 9), and cooking (chapter 10). If you have gardening experience you can easily skip the parts of the book that you're familiar with and go directly to what's new to you. You can also use the index to focus on the information that is most important to you.

I'm going to begin with a description of a plant that some people call a lifesaver and others call a weed.

Marijuana in Amsterdam. An ancient plant in an ancient botanical garden, the Hortus Botanicus Amsterdam, established in 1638. Down the street in coffeehouses, people are smoking this plant's relatives.

CHAPTER 1

Marijuana Renegade

That Ever-Adaptable Rank, Weedy Annual

A favorite book in my library is *Weeds of the West*, a 630-page encyclopedia originally published in 1992 by the prestigious Western Society of Weed Science at the University of Wyoming. Instead of adopting just any common definition of a weed, like a wild plant growing where it is not wanted and in competition with cultivated plants, the society takes the high road and says that a weed is "a plant that interferes with management objectives for a given area of land at a given point in time." And then they further explain that "the term 'weed' does not always indicate that a plant is totally undesirable, or that it cannot be beneficial under certain situations."

Marijuana is given two pages in full color; these weed specialists don't warn of any potential dangers of the plant and merely observe that it has "a peculiar odor," noting that it was once a crop used in the West for rope making. In other words, it's just another plant, like western wild cucumber or prairie onion, which sometimes interferes with the objectives of land managers like farmers. Tell that to the DEA.

The famous ethnobotanist, Richard Evans Schultes, observes in his book *Hallucinogenic Plants* (Golden Press, 1976), "It is well recognized that *Cannabis sativa* is one of man's oldest cultivated plants." I don't have the space here to document

marijuana's origin and influence on humankind, but I will tell you that the plant has had some very famous supporters.

The "founding father farmers" of the United States were big hemp fans. Thomas Jefferson proclaimed, "Hemp is of first necessity to the wealth and protection of the country," with George Washington chiming in, "Make the most you can of the Indian Hemp seed and sow it everywhere." These comments were inspired by the high quality of hemp rope, which itself has a long and distinguished history, mostly because of the ropes and lines used on sailing vessels for centuries. The hemp fiber was also used to make coarse cloth, burlap, twine, and paper.

Hemp seed contains a greenish-yellow oil that's rich in unsaturated fatty acids. In the past, it was used as lamp fuel, varnish, a substitute for linseed oil in artists' oil paints, and as a bird food. The seeds were not commonly known as a food for humans, but they are high in protein (25 to 33 percent) and were eaten during famines in China. In India, the seeds are combined with amaranth or rice to make a grain dish called *mura*.

In addition, a substantial worldwide hemp industry produces fabric, twine and cord, bags, socks, sweaters, yarn, body-care products, hemp seed oil, hemp foodstuffs made from the seeds and their oil (lollipops, snack bars, pasta, and bread), and pet food. The list of hemp products is seemingly endless, but my favorite is an electric car that has been built out of hemp.

Beyond hemp, there are the healing aspects of marijuana. Medical marijuana references are found on several Egyptian papyri dating as far back as 1700 BCE, and Leo likes to point out that the ancient Egyptians used cannabis in suppositories for relieving the pain of hemorrhoids. But the archaeological find that intrigues me the most is dated to 2,700 years ago: the world's oldest stash of high-potency marijuana, found in the tomb of a Gūshī shaman in China's Xinjiang Province. Nearly two pounds of cleaned marijuana was found in the tomb, and the sample lacked large stems and male flowers, indicating, according to an article about the discovery, "removal by

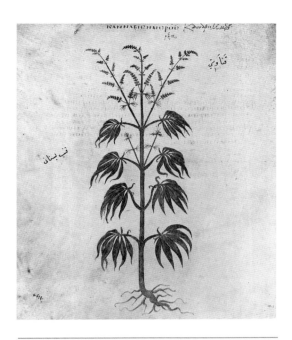

An early sixth-century illuminated manuscript of *De Materia Medica*, by Dioscorides. The Arabic words at left appear to be *qinnab bustani*, or "garden hemp."

human intervention" because those plant parts are "pharmacologically less psychoactive" ("Phytochemical and genetic analyses of ancient cannabis from Central Asia," by Ethan B. Russo, et al., *Journal of Experimental Botany*, 2008).

Irish doctor William O'Shaughnessy was the first major proponent for marijuana's medical use in England and America. A physician with the British East India Company, he found that marijuana eased the pain of rheumatism and was helpful at relieving discomfort and nausea in cases of rabies, cholera, and tetanus. Later, of course, the tide turned and marijuana was considered by various governments to be as dangerous as heroin or cocaine. It wasn't until the late twentieth and early twenty-first

centuries that the tide turned again and certain states—along with about twenty countries, including Canada, Mexico, Ecuador, Argentina, and Israel—legalized marijuana's use "for medicinal purposes." Despite what some states permit, the federal statutes against its cultivation and possession have remained in effect.

But one of the most interesting facts about marijuana is unrelated to any medical properties and involves its self-reproduction. Unlike many domesticated plants and crops that cannot reproduce on their own and depend on humankind (like corn and my domesticated chile peppers), marijuana is a renegade plant that escaped from cultivation and is perfectly capable of thriving on its own, thank you very much. A maverick, for you cowboy growers out there, and a marvel of adaptability.

Left, This is how medical marijuana is sold by dispensaries in California.

Right, A wide variety of snacks and treats can be used to dispense edible medical marijuana.

The Survivalist Plant

Marijuana is a survivor. It grows easily everywhere in the world except in arctic climes and can live at elevations up to 8,000 feet. Its seeds germinate easily and quickly in about six days, and two weeks later it is so established that it can grow two to five inches a day, depending on the variety and the growing conditions. It is incredibly tolerant of poor soils, and it doesn't need as much water as some growers believe it does. Wild marijuana plants are vigorous, aggressive, and competitive weeds—if I'm allowed to use that debatable term. Some varieties have large root systems that enable them to survive low-water stress and poor soil. Wild marijuana has been found from Union Square in New York City to lower Alaska.

Most experts attribute the adaptability of marijuana to two factors: wind pollination and the fact that the plants are *dioecious,* meaning that there are separate male and female plants—exactly like mulberry trees. Both of these factors promote diversity and *hybridization* (the cross-breeding of different varieties), resulting in *hybrid vigor,* which is an increase in the performance of hybrids over that of purebred plants. In the case of marijuana, this means larger plants with greater flower production and often more powerful flowers.

But what kind of a plant is it? To sum up some observations, it's a woody, weedy annual with a very strong aroma when it flowers. It's also highly variable, ranging from one species less than a foot tall to another that's more than fifteen times that height.

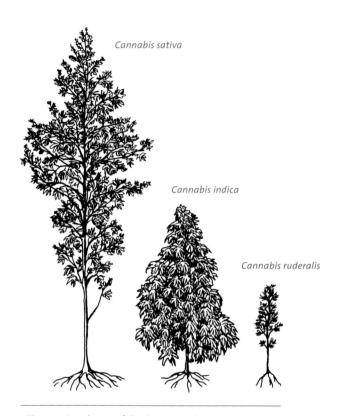

Cannabis sativa

Cannabis indica

Cannabis ruderalis

The growing shapes of the three cannabis species.

The Three True Species

The history of marijuana's botanical classification is long and murky, but I think it has pretty much been resolved these days. After extended and intense bickering over technicalities about subspecies versus true species, in 1974 Richard Evans Schultes, W. M. Klein, T. Plowman, and T. E. Lockwood, in their breakthrough study "Cannabis: An Example of Taxonomic Neglect," published by the Botanical Museum, Harvard University, proclaimed that there were, indeed, three species of cannabis that can be cross-bred, further increasing the adaptability of the

The familiar leaf of the most ubiquitous species, *Cannabis sativa.*

The wider leaf of "skunky" *Cannabis indica.*

The odd-shaped leaf of the autoflowering *Cannabis ruderalis.*

plant. Of course, writers, growers, and armchair botanists are still debating about marijuana speciation, but I'm here to say it doesn't matter because taxonomy is not our concern here. I am assuming that Schultes and his colleagues are correct and that we are dealing with three species.

Cannabis sativa

Cannabis sativa, the most familiar species, grows the tallest of the three and averages between four and fifteen feet. It has long *internodes* (spaces between the branches) of four to six inches. The *palmate* (shaped like a hand) leaves are long, thin, and very pointed with six to twelve *leaflets* (small leaves) per compound leaf (a leaf composed of numerous leaflets) and are solid green with no markings. Because they grow so large, they typically produce the most amount (by weight) of flowering tops, but their size is a drawback to home growers like Leo, who must prune his *sativa* plants weekly.

All *hemp* varieties—nonpsychoactive cannabis grown for its fiber—are believed to be *sativa,* but that differentiation is murky

because some experts now think that *C. ruderalis* is an escaped *sativa* hemp variety that evolved into a new species. I mention this because, as we will see later, hybrids of *sativa* or *indica* with *ruderalis* have produced plants that are perfect for container gardening under lights in small areas, like the closet grow room mentioned in chapter 3.

Cannabis indica

Cannabis indica is a much smaller species than *sativa,* usually with a maximum height of about four feet. It has shorter internodes between the branches and its leaves are wide and short with marbled patterns on them and just three to five leaflets per leaf. The *indica* varieties grow faster than the *sativa* varieties and their flower tops have more THC (tetrahydrocannabinol, the active ingredient in marijuana) in them. They are preferred by medical growers because they are more potent medicinally. This species and a subspecies of *sativa,* *C. afghanica,* are the principal marijuana plants used to make hashish.

Some *indica* varieties have an unpleasant odor like that of skunk spray or cat urine, while others have a pleasant aroma. The skunky odor is the result of *terpenes* (smelly organic compounds) in the resinous flower tops that are similar to the resin of pine trees, hence turpentine, from which the word *terpene* is derived. Terpenes are *phytotoxins* produced by the plant to protect itself, such as urushiol in poison ivy, which repels mammals and keeps them from eating its seeds. In the flowering tops of *indica, sativa,* and their hybrids, specifically, the resin has *diterpenes*, a specific form of terpene that can block and deter insect feeding. The *indica* diterpene's smell closely resembles the sulfurous odor of skunk spray caused by chemicals called *mercaptans*, so they become the herbaceous skunks of botany.

Cannabis ruderalis

Cannabis ruderalis is the bad boy for growers because it produces little or no THC, precisely like hemp. That problem gave it a predictably bad reputation until breeders realized that *ruderalis* had a unique trait involving *photoperiodism* (the initiation of flowering in response to relative lengths of day and night). For *sativa* and *indica*, flowering is triggered by the shorter days and longer nights of the coming fall, which is called a shorter photoperiod. *Ruderalis* flowering is not dependent upon photoperiod, but rather on its maturity. In a little more than a month of growing, most *ruderalis* plants begin to bloom. It skips the usual *vegetative growth periods* (plant growing before flowering). This trait, combined with its short stature—it rarely exceeds three feet in height—caused breeders to wonder if *ruderalis-indica* hybrids could be developed for home growers. Thus the variety 'Lowryder' was born, and that hybrid became one of Leo's favorite plants. "It's very easy to grow," he told me, "and perfect for stealth growing because the tallest 'Lowryder' I've grown was only twenty-three inches." That said, I've seen one of Leo's *ruderalis-sativa* hybrids and he's constantly trimming it back to keep it at six feet tall. This happens because marijuana

Cannabis ruderalis growing near Saratov City, Russia. This nonpsychoactive species is what *sativa* and *indica* were crossed with to produce autoflowering varieties.

breeding (just like the breeding of any other plant) is not an exact science and the hybrid is also affected by growing conditions such as the amount of fertilizer it is receiving.

Cannabis ruderalis leaves have three to six leaflets and are small, thick, and lack THC just like the flowers. So there's no real reason to grow this *ditch weed*, a slang term for a useless marijuana plant. However, the hybrids are very small plants at maturity, so they're perfect for growing under lights. With the lights set at twenty-four-hours-on per day, sprouting to harvest takes just two months for most of the hybrids, and the yields are good for such midget plants. They do, however, count in your permissible state limit for the total number of medicinal plants. For details on these hybrids, see chapter 4.

The Tragic Life Cycle of a Healing Herb

Plants that have served humankind for millennia are regarded fondly by their growers, and some become quasi pets. The hibiscus plants on my front patio are at least thirty-five years old and still bloom nicely after they recover from low-light wintering-over in my greenhouse. It sounds weird, but like dogs and cats, certain favorite perennial plants become part of the family. Not so with marijuana, probably because its life cycle is so short that you don't have time to become attached to individual plants. As annuals, they are programmed to flourish, flower, and die—all within a few months.

Here's how it happens:

Germination, the simple sprouting of a seed, starts the process. Marijuana seeds are quick to sprout once they are provided with moisture and warmth. Some marijuana seeds sprout in less than a day, but the average time is typically five or six days. Because the seeds are so expensive—particularly the exotic hybrids—you should study the various germination techniques described in chapter 5 and decide which works best for you.

The **seedling stage** begins when you place the sprouted seed root-down in the initial growing medium. The first leaves to appear are the round, smooth embryonic leaves and they are quickly followed by initial, tiny serrated leaves. It is important to provide the seedlings with close, intense light. Otherwise, they will get *leggy* (they extend themselves to reach the light) and fall over. Brisk air circulation from a fan will move the slight stems around, toughening them. Note that this is the most vulnerable stage for your marijuana plant during its lifetime. Seedlings are defenseless against pets like cats, which will munch on them, insect infestations such as aphids, and especially damping-off disease. (For more about this malady, see chapters 5 and 9.) Inspect the seedlings carefully at least once a day and don't let them ever dry out.

Vegetative growth starts when the seedling has a minimum of three sets of leaves and is transferred to its three-gallon home. As Leo knows from his *sativa* experiences, this growth gets more dramatic over time and, depending upon the lighting in the growing

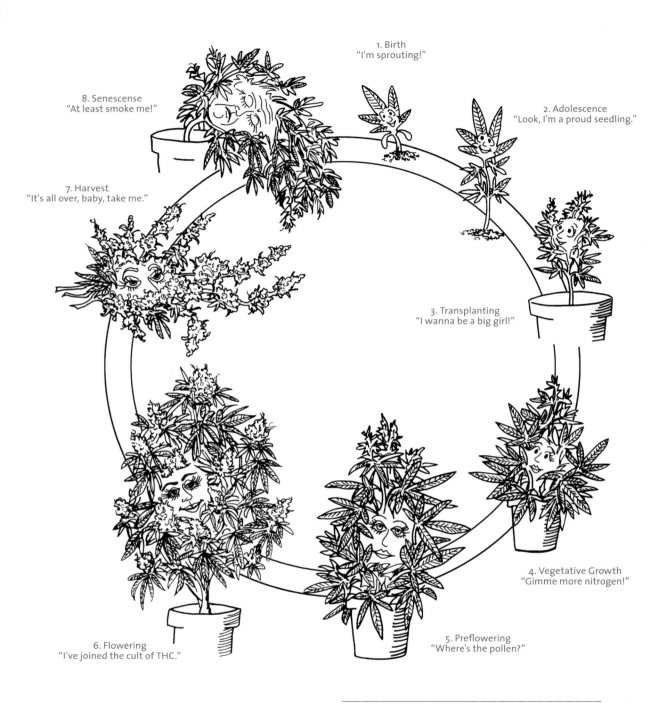

The cannabis life cycle: From germination to senescence, a short, weedy existence.

environment, even spectacular. Some plants require constant pruning (discussed in chapter 7) prior to flowering—be sure to keep all the trimmed leaf as it can be used in cooking (see chapter 10). The vegetative growth can last anywhere from one to five months, depending upon the variety, the environment, and whether or not you induce early flowering.

Preflowering begins when vertical growth slows and the plant starts to fill in with more branches and *nodes*, the points where the branches meet the stem. A *calyx* (or nub, or pod, or bud—the terminology varies) will form in the nodes, and will develop into either male or female flowers. If you are growing for *sinsemilla* (Spanish for "without seed")—that is, growing for just the unpollinated flowering tops, which is the goal of the medical grower—the appearance of male flowers means only one thing: the offending plant must be terminated. If you are growing for seed, you will need the male pollen, so keep the plant. Males usually show their gender before females, so keep one male plant and isolate it until it's mature so it won't pollinate your entire crop. You can even collect the pollen and freeze it for later use. Destroy any other male plants.

Flowering can last from four to eight weeks and ends with the production of seeds or when the *sinsemilla* tops reach their optimum growth and have started to slow. Contrary to popular slang, *buds* are not flowering tops. The true buds, as mentioned previously, are the beginning of the flowering process, not the end of it. In fact, here is the original definition, written in a dictionary of botanical terms in 1879 that has no mention of flowers: "*Bud*. The undeveloped state of a stem or branch, with or without leaves." Nowadays, the term "bud" means a nodule that can turn into a leaf, a branching stem, or a flower. The peak of flowering marijuana means maximum aroma, so keep that in mind as the flowers mature. The *trichomes*, resin-secreting plant hairs, will glisten as the resin builds up and will feel sticky to the touch. This is a good thing because it indicates your plants are producing THC and are nearing their peak of development.

Harvest and death go hand in hand with marijuana plants. As annuals, their time is finite and there will be no wintering-over for them. In nature, after the flowering produces seeds, the plant enters *senescence*, which means a decline toward death. But since it's depressing to watch a plant wither away and die when you can do nothing to extend its life, it's better to end everything quickly. Harvest, trim, and begin curing the flower tops. Remove all the other leaves, plus the trimmed top leaves, and add them to your trim-drying box. (All of these topics are covered in chapter 8.). And then start the germination process again.

In subsequent chapters I cover all the details for these stages and procedures, but I wanted everyone to have an initial overview of what's to come. Now it's time to take a look at the options for marijuana growing locations.

CHAPTER 2

Security

First and Foremost

Security for your growing operation is the most important aspect of the marijuana garden. Experienced growers believe that bragging and gossiping about your crop causes nearly all security problems. It makes complete sense that the fewer the number of people who know about your growing operation, the more secure it will be. It's not that your friends are going to raid your garden plot, it's a matter of their lips saying to others, "I just tried some of that *sinsemilla* that John is growing, and wow!" That's all it takes for your plants to be targeted, so it is in your best interest to severely limit the number of people who know what you are doing, regardless of the fact that you're growing them legally.

Some expert growers are even more rigorous about security and urge growers to tell no one, and to never trust anyone, including parents, siblings, spouses, and children. These concepts are great in theory, but hardly practical. Families are often close and very observant of the activities of their immediate relatives. If your marijuana garden is in your basement, it's going to be a little difficult to hide it from your spouse and relatives who want to see it. Just use common sense and don't tell anyone who doesn't need to know.

Here's what can happen if you're a careless grower. It's a true story. In mid-March of 1995, I was writing on the computer when I heard the Dobermans going nuts in the backyard, and soon there was a loud banging on the front door. I opened it and greeted two long-haired guys with a fifteen-year-old Dodge in the driveway. They both reached into their pockets and pulled out badges.

"New Mexico State Police," said one.

"DEA," said the other.

"Come on in—it's been twenty-five years since I had a visit from the narcs," I joked. "And back then I had long hair and they had the wrong apartment."

They looked a little embarrassed and the state cop asked, "Are you a writer or something?" He'd obviously done a background check on me.

"Yes, I'm the editor of *Chile Pepper* magazine."

"I thought so," he said, eyeing his partner. "It had to be something like that."

"What's this all about?" I asked.

"Well," replied the cop, "we have to check out all the reports we get, no matter how crazy they are."

"Is this about capsaicin?" I interrupted.

"What's that? No, someone told us you were growing marijuana."

I laughed. "Not quite."

The DEA agent chimed in. "You've got a heated greenhouse with just the roof transparent," he accused, "and it's guarded by Dobermans."

"Damn right," I said, "so let's go have a look."

The cop glanced at DEA again and shook his head. I took them through the kitchen and laundry room and into my ramshackle greenhouse, where I showed them my just-sprouted habanero seedlings.

"Chile peppers," said the cop, chuckling. The agent blushed, totally embarrassed. "We're real sorry, Mr. DeWitt," he told me as they left.

I gave my farewell: "Thanks for coming without a warrant and tear gas." But I was thinking, You're five years too late.

Later, when my wife—whose given name is, ironically, Mary Jane—returned, she wondered who had falsely turned us in. "Maybe we burned somebody out at the Fiery Foods Show," she suggested.

That triggered it for me. The show. All the stuff from the show under our carport, ready for shipping. And there it was, the clearly marked box containing the large high-intensity discharge lamp from the New Earth Garden Center display in plain sight from the street. The people at New Earth had shipped me the grow light for an indoor pepper growing display, and after the show I had stored it temporarily under the carport. I guess a meter reader had seen it, noticed my secure greenhouse, the Dobermans "guarding" it, and had concluded that I was growing 'Rio Grande Wowee.' He was duty bound to report it to the proper authorities, and so on. No Crime Stoppers reward for that guy! Mystery solved. Or so we think.

My attorney, a rather outspoken guy, was furious with me when I told him. "You should have refused to let them in unless they had a warrant," he said. "You should have called me immediately and let me handle it."

"But I had nothing to hide," I protested.

"No matter. You can't let the police search your house without a warrant."

"They didn't search it—I just let them see my chile plants."

He insisted on reading me the riot act about my rights, but I still think that I did the right thing. Forcing them to get a warrant would just make them mad, and I had heard of law enforcement officers planting drugs on people they didn't like. Besides, I didn't want my house torn apart. They were gone, and I didn't have to pay my lawyer.

An experience like this, plus a nongovernment raid on a growing operation I was involved with, has made me very conservative when it comes to security for marijuana gardens. I don't want to discourage you before you even start growing, but you've got to be realistic about what you're doing: marijuana is a very valuable crop that generates billions of dollars for a mostly underground economy. I want everyone to be a successful grower, but I don't want anyone facing a weapon or a possible prison term. So keep that in mind as you review the security of your garden, based upon the following factors, which you should check off, one by one.

- Location: Grow in a place that is naturally and easily secured.

- Protection: Go beyond just location and protect your garden further with other methods. There are many, ranging from very simple to complicated.

- Outside Interaction: Protect yourself and your garden by using discretion when dealing with the real world.

- Camouflage: Incorporate measures to disguise any cultivation methods that might reveal your garden to others. Three senses are involved here—sight, sound, and smell.

- Busted: Know that you're never as secure as you think you are.

Am I being paranoid? Maybe, but I think a better term would be very cautious. Now let's take a closer look at each of the items on the checklist.

Location, Location, Location

Regardless of whether your marijuana garden is indoors, outdoors, or both, your first consideration must be access. Besides you, who else could possibly have access to your plants? This factor is the reason why a marijuana garden on your own property is the only real option for growing legally, because—with the exception of a search warrant from the authorities—you will have total control over accessibility. A rented house with an absentee owner is the next best option, but even then you run the risk of someone appearing at your front door saying, "I just bought this house from the previous owner, and I'm here to do an inspection because I want to resell it as soon as possible." Do not even *think* about growing marijuana in an apartment complex as tempting as it may be. Too many people have access there; the heat, odor, noise, and ventilation produced by indoor cultivation can give you away no matter how cleverly they are disguised.

Ideally, your grow house, as I will call it, should be in a somewhat remote area. A long, private driveway with a high gate that can be locked would be excellent, as would a backyard with a wall—not a mere fence—but a wall six feet high made of cinderblock with two-foot-high privacy extensions on top of it made of wood or fiberglass. It's relatively easy to climb over a six-foot wall, but the extensions make it much more difficult and noisy. The wall should have a sturdy, eight-foot-high wooden gate with internal and external padlocks. A wall system like this will give you a good measure of privacy, except from helicopters and satellites, of course. But if you're growing legally, those nuisances probably will not bother you. Still, you can disguise your plants from overhead surveillance by using intercropping techniques, which I'll discuss in chapter 3.

A greenhouse or other structure in a walled yard can also be used as a growing area, especially if it's disguised as a tool shed or even a small barn. I have used a large metal building that was built to look like a storage barn, but every other panel on the roof and the side facing south was made from translucent fiberglass, which in effect turned it into a disguised greenhouse. I could have opted for all the roof panels and south-facing panels to be fiberglass, and the plants would have produced more, but that would have given away the fact that the structure was a greenhouse. At that time, with horses on the property, it just looked like a well-lit horse barn.

If you decide to have an indoor garden in your home, you have several options. You can build a special room for growing, or simply devote a spare room in your house for that purpose. The best option is an attic, basement, or retrofitted closet, areas where guests would never go. Of course, all of these indoor options would need adequate ventilation and electricity. I go into a lot more detail on the construction of indoor grow rooms in chapter 3. One thing to think about before you begin building a grow room is that the lights and fans will necessitate increased electricity use, so it's a good idea to invent a cover story in case anyone notices. A friend of a friend of mine has an electric kiln and makes pottery for her cover story.

Some adventurous growers (or stupid fools, as the case may be) indulge in outdoor "guerrilla gardening," where they attempt to grow their crop on the property of other people or in state or national parks. This kind of growing operation requires not only taking great risks but also a massive deployment of resources, expenses, time, and effort. It's certainly not legal and you always take the chance that someone will stumble across it, or wait until you've done all the hard work and then raid the operation and steal the harvest. My advice? Don't even consider this option—it's much too dangerous.

To summarize location selection, first you should own the property. Although a remote location in the country is preferable to a city site, you can make either work. Ideally there should be no tall buildings nearby, like offices or apartments where someone could spy on you from above. A high fence or wall is a necessity to keep people and animals out of your growing area. Gas, water, and electricity meters should never be in a growing area. If indoors, your garden should be in the most remote and inaccessible part of your house, like a basement or attic.

Protecting Your Growing Area

To determine the type and degree of protection your garden might need, you must thoroughly evaluate the location based upon accessibility. You must also keep in mind that certain security devices and procedures are so obvious that they could give you away by their very presence. Thieves will not waste their time breaking into a house that has nothing valuable, and dead giveaways that you are protecting something worth stealing are security company signs plastered everywhere, obvious security cameras on poles, and any kind of fortification, like bars on windows and doors. Remember, you're aiming for normality here—your house or farm must seem average and bland, just like all the others in your neighborhood. It should not stand out in any way. Pit bulls in your backyard are completely over-the-top when a single Chihuahua would be much more effective as an alarm and not draw any undue attention.

I have toured the backyard growing operation of someone even more cautious than I am, and this person believes that technology is the answer to security. You must decide if you need his level of protection or not. He has mounted floodlights on the right and left corners of the bottom of the roof facing his backyard. In the middle of the bottom of the roof he has mounted a closed-circuit TV camera with a built-in microphone that uploads the video images to his home computer or his smartphone and records them. He also has installed a motion-detection sensor system to not only turn on the lights and camera but also to trigger an alarm of wailing sirens. His theory about this level of protection is that he wants to scare off intruders and record who they are. You'll have to research this level of security for your particular setup, but if you want to go through with it, start with Dakota Alert, which makes some reasonably priced motion detection sensors that detect humans but not small animals. The device should be hidden in the middle of the yard and ideally could be engineered to start the camera and turn on the lights simultaneously. This way, even if you're gone when a raid happens, at least the lights and siren will scare off the intruders or alert the neighbors to call the cops. Anyway, the intruders won't have time to track down all the plants hidden in the yard. If it works, you'll have a YouTube video that will go viral!

If you want to go down this road, Secure Sight makes a very handy, three-in-one security unit that includes a 500-watt floodlight with a three megapixel digital camera with a time and date stamp for still photos, and a digital video recorder with a 512-megabyte SD card.

The system has a motion detector built into it, plus a USB cable for connecting it to your computer. The unit is self-contained, weighs only four pounds, and can be installed in minutes. It costs a mere $149 and is available from www.northerntool.com.

I think this level of security is excessive and if an alarm is triggered, what are the ramifications? Even if you're growing legally, you have just announced to the world that you have something very valuable on your property, and you probably have compromised the location for further growing. Let's go for simpler security solutions.

I know growers who live in their own houses in urban areas but who have to take extra measures for the sake of security, like high walls around the backyard and strong locks on the gates (both inside and outside). Some growers post "Beware of Dog" signs in place of burglar alarm signs, even if they don't actually own a fierce dog. One step you can take inexpensively is to make sure that your house lights are on timers if you are away overnight. In every way, the house and yard appear normal. And normal is what you want everything to be to avoid attention and possible suspicion.

Growing marijuana is not worth anyone getting hurt, so forget about using booby traps or any other protection devices that might injure someone. That said, you don't want your crop stolen, and that must be your first priority, so if you're growing legally and have the proper documentation, the police will not confiscate your plants.

As mentioned above, some growers have used aggressive animals for securing their operations, including pit bulls, bears, and alligators (I'm not kidding), but you don't have to go to that extreme. Think poodle, because the best protection you can have is a dog. I'm not suggesting an attack dog, because, once again, someone could get hurt and it could be you or a loved one, or your dog if there were an actual home dope invasion in progress. All you want is a dog that spends most of its time in the yard so it is protective of its territory and barks furiously at passersby. Suggested breeds are Chihuahuas, terriers, and small mutts. Yes, there will be plenty of false alarms, mostly due to cats, but when your dog goes nuts barking, just remind yourself that he's simply doing his job.

If you are growing inside your house, be sure to routinely lock the door to your growing area. Once I used a secure basement with no windows for my indoor plantation, and I was very tempted to put a padlock on the door. But since the door was adjacent to the kitchen, where people tend to congregate, a padlock would draw unnecessary attention to the door. Rather, I just used the lock on the door, which took an old-fashioned skeleton key. If anyone asked what the door led to, I would say, "That goes to the messiest storage room in the city," and that would always end the conversation. I should point out here that my appearance at the time, as well as the appearance of the house, was as normal as possible because I didn't want to stand out.

Outside Interaction: Be Mr. or Ms. Normal

No matter what your political or personal beliefs may be, when you're a marijuana grower, the appearance of normality is a necessity. Who is going to look more suspicious: a conventional-looking citizen with a short haircut driving a Toyota Corolla or a long-haired, tattooed guy riding a Harley with a "Legalize It" sticker? So be that good citizen and don't do anything that would attract attention to you or alert your neighbors that you might be a problem to them. Be nice but avoid unnecessary socializing. Be the quiet neighbor who waves and says hi, doesn't block their cars, and has his animals confined to his own property. Forget throwing parties with blaring music that will cause the neighbors to complain to the police.

Have a real job so you're not hanging around the house all day. Since I've always been a writer, I have used that cover to explain the days when I'm home, although that's rarely asked if you've reached retirement age. Use some of the time at home to keep your house and yard looking good, always repaired and painted.

Remember that your trash can give you away if someone is suspicious. Be sure to separate your grow-room trash from your normal household trash. Keep it in a separate garbage bag and make certain that nothing in that bag can be traced to you, like a bank or credit card statement or an electricity bill. When the bag is full, don't place it with your other trash, but put it into a cardboard box and put it in the trunk of your car. Find an unlocked dumpster somewhere and make a midnight deposit.

Lights, bulbs, and ballast for the indoor grow room should be purchased from local shops rather than by mail order.

Back in the days when I was growing, I could not afford the expensive high-intensity discharge (HID) lights that were made for industrial use, so I bought simple two-bulb, four-foot fluorescent fixtures equipped with Vita-Lite bulbs that closely imitated natural sunlight. Today if I used them, I would be laughed out of the Marijuana Growers Association, but they did work and I didn't have to worry about my equipment purchase incriminating me. If you are growing legally, this won't be a problem in the states that permit growing, but still, use the same caution as you would if your plants were not legal.

Do not use mail-order suppliers for equipment because then you become part of a database that can be subpoenaed by federal or even state agents. Instead, buy locally. In every moderately large city there are specialty shops that sell indoor grow lights and hydroponic equipment for "hobbyists." Of course, the owners of these shops know that most of the equipment they are selling will be used for growing marijuana, but most of them will not admit it publicly or to customers. In fact, if you mention marijuana in some of these shops, you will be escorted out the door. If they ask what you are going to use the lights for, you are, of course, growing chile peppers indoors during the winter. Being prudent, you will, obviously, pay for all purchases in good old untraceable cash. If they ask you to join their mailing list, pleasantly decline the offer.

Some of the more paranoid (or extremely cautious) growers suggest that you borrow someone else's car when you go to purchase your lights or other equipment, which presumes that the antidrug authorities have every single garden hobby shop under constant surveillance. This is unlikely, and using a friend's car is unfair to the friend (unless you've told your friend what's going on, which you're not supposed to do anyway). Just use caution and common sense, and you'll be fine.

A corollary to caution and common sense is to hide your plants as much as possible.

The marijuana garden. Here's what I want your garden to look like, with marijuana as a companion to your other plants.

Camouflage

Hiding marijuana plants growing outdoors is not as difficult as you think if the garden is on your property. The two basic ways to accomplish this are within a structure or among other plants that resemble marijuana in growing habit, leaf shape, and bloom shape.

Stealth Structures and Plants for Security

As mentioned, I have used a storage barn that functioned as a greenhouse because of a translucent roof—so think tool shed, cold frame (a sun-heated board frame covered with a removable top of glass or other transparent material and sunk into the ground), or some other structure that fits in well with the design of your yard.

One of the cleverest structures I've seen is variously called an *urban garden* or a *covered raised bed*, and consists simply of a raised bed usually made with 1 by 6-inch or 1 by 8-inch redwood boards for the base, and a half-moon-shaped, hinged cover made from plastic tubing and a white, translucent cloth called DeWitt N-Sulate (no relation to me) available from online gardening equipment suppliers. This cloth is opaque from the outside but admits 75 to 80 percent of sunlight, resulting in beautifully diffused light that is perfect for growing marijuana. (During hot weather, you will have to prop open the bottom of the row cover about a foot to reduce the temperature of the bed and increase air circulation.) The urban garden is also useful for protecting your plants from most insects, snails, wind, hail, and varmints such as mice and cats. I mention cats because they will munch on marijuana seedlings in the same way they eat lawn grass, and this will cause vomiting. With the plants so concealed, you can even bring people into your backyard without much apprehension. Of course, some curious folks will ask what the structure is, and you can tell them it's your winter herb garden and you'd show it to them but the hinges are broken and you haven't repaired them yet.

I love the idea of hiding marijuana plants in plain sight by mixing them with plants that have a similar appearance. Not only does this method confuse the eye of the untrained, casual viewer, but also many of the similar plants have beautiful foliage and flowers that attract hummingbirds and butterflies. Like marijuana, these plants have palmately compound leaves (roughly shaped like a human hand with multiple leaflets per leaf) and some have bloom stalks that somewhat resemble the flowering tops of marijuana.

During one summer growing season, the stealth plants around Leo's front and back yards were concealed so well that I never noticed them. The key here is that I wasn't searching for them. If no one knows you're growing marijuana, then visitors won't be looking for it. They tend to notice bright, colorful flowers to the point that they don't pay any attention to the palmate foliage concealed within the flowering plants. Leo showed me a stealth plant I never noticed and said it had been in the same position in his front yard for weeks and that his wife, who does the watering in their traditional garden, never saw it either. But if Leo had challenged either one of us to play marijuana hide and seek, we would have found them quickly. Note that all the stealth plants are the short ones. It's obviously much more difficult to conceal a six-foot-tall *sativa*. The smaller plants, like 'Lowryder #2', can thrive in containers smaller than three gallons, which means you can also crowd more plants into a given area.

Skunky Plants

One giveaway that you are growing marijuana either indoors or outdoors is the aroma produced by flowering tops, especially the *indica* varieties with their signature "skunky" odor. Many people, of course, won't recognize the smell or associate it with marijuana, but some will. The covering used in the urban garden for outside growing (mentioned on page 29) will contain some of the smell, but you still have to lift the cover up to water the plants, so it's best to do that in the afternoon, when breezes are stronger and will dissipate the odor rapidly. You can also use cedar shavings, not bark, for mulch in your entire garden. Cedar can somewhat disguise the smell of flowering tops, but not entirely. If you are worried about the odor of your outdoor plants, ask your seed supplier for less-smelly varieties, especially the smaller *indica-sativa* hybrids. Generally speaking, *indica* varieties are smaller and more compact, thus easier to conceal than the nonskunky

Leo built his own grow bed, designed after some sold commercially in the city where he lives.

sativas, which tend to grow very large. But many *indicas* have the skunky aroma, so you have a bit of a quandary here. More information about choosing varieties is covered in chapter 4.

If some of your plants become really smelly as the flowering tops mature, some may have to be sacrificed by harvesting them earlier than desired. All growers or farmers of any kind of plant occasionally have to make such decisions—it's simply a part of agriculture.

If you are growing indoors and a dinner guest asks if you have a pet skunk, you know you have a serious problem. Are you venting your grow room properly? Probably not. You

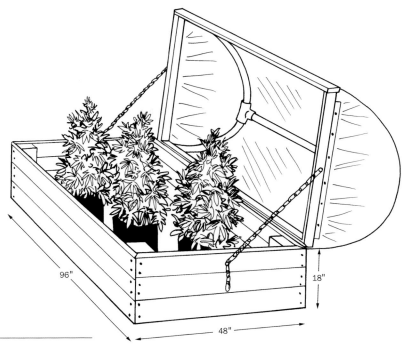

These are the suggested dimensions for building your own grow bed.

can also buy devices to reduce indoor odors, such as deodorizers, ozone and ion generators, and activated charcoal filters, but your venting system should be your first line of defense. All of this is discussed in more detail in the next chapter, but you should have odors in mind before you begin, because they are definitely a security issue.

The Grid Knows All— Sometimes

I have mentioned inventing a cover story to explain the use of additional electricity for an indoor grow room, but that's only a part of the electricity usage story. Some growers suggest that you keep your usage about the same as

it was before the grow room was constructed by disconnecting the clothes dryer or turning down the thermostat of your electric water heater and furnace. All of these remedies imply an illegal grow room. If you are growing legally, it won't make any difference if your electricity usage increases, but electricity use brings an additional security issue: the danger of fire because of improperly wired lights, vents, and fans—especially in proximity to water.

I never had any trouble with this when I was using fluorescent fixtures, but today's lighting systems are more powerful, demand more electricity, and become much hotter during use. As you are planning your grow room, determine what kind of outlets you will need and make sure that they meet your local

The average guest would not notice the marijuana plant amid the profusion of *Vitex*.

From a distance, bur marigold resembles marijuana. Up close, you can see that the leaves are different from marijuana leaves because they are not palmate, but rather pinnate (featherlike), and the flowers do not resemble marijuana tops.

Chaste tree or **monk's pepper** *(Vitex agnus-castus)* is one of the best plants to use to camouflage marijuana plants. Its leaves closely match marijuana, and plants concealed in a dense stand of *Vitex* could not be detected unless you were close enough to touch them.

I mistook a preflowering clump of **bur marigold** *(Bidens aristosa)* growing in an irrigation drain for a marijuana plant until I inspected it closely. Also called by the odd name "nodding beggartick," this plant is a weed or a wildflower (depending on your view), but you would have to find some in the wild and harvest their seeds to use them. And they are not nearly as attractive as *Vitex* or **lupines**, which have similar leaves and a *pedicle* (stalk of an individual flower) fairly similar to the flowering tops of marijuana.

A marijuana plant concealed in **monarda**—a bushy plant with dense foliage—was just six feet from Leo's front door, and neither his wife nor I ever noticed it.

Monarda.

Bamboo.

Bottlebrush buckeye *(Aesculus parviflora)* would also be an excellent flowering plant for concealing marijuana. The dense habit of the plant makes an effective screen.

Although **golden bamboo** *(Phyllostachys aurea)* is invasive and difficult to control, if your marijuana plants were concealed within or behind a tall stand of it they would be virtually undetectable. Leo uses this variety (which is called *running* or *spreading* bamboo), but varieties of clumping bamboo, such as **umbrella bamboo** *(Fargesia murielae)*, do not spread and would work better.

In vegetable gardens, the most commonly used concealing plant is **corn** *(Zea mays)*. By intercropping marijuana amid the taller corn stalks, you can effectively disguise your marijuana garden during the summer growing months. Large tomato plants can also be used if they are a barrier and the marijuana plants are concealed behind their closely planted, dense growth. More details about companion flowers and vegetables can be found in chapter 3.

Corn or maize.

electrical code. You can even hire an electrician to do this without divulging what you are going to be doing. You just tell the electrician that you're going to sell the house and want an inspection to make sure the electrical system meets the local code. Then read about the requirements of the growing components on the equipment you are going to buy, including the installation procedures. The more you read and the more you learn, the safer your grow room will be.

If you're really concerned about increased electricity use revealing your indoor grow room, you can put dwarf marijuana varieties under compact fluorescent lights (CFLs) alone. A full-spectrum, 125-watt CFL on a vegetative growth light cycle of eighteen hours on and six hours off will not increase your electric bill noticeably. I'll talk more about lighting options in chapter 3.

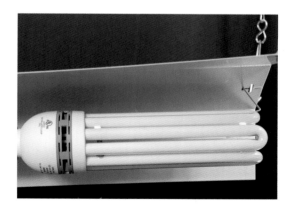

Compact fluorescent lights are excellent for growing seedlings or small, autoflowering varieties.

Busted: Caught in the Act

If someone really wants to breach your security, they can at will and there's practically nothing you can do to stop it.

A trailer custom-made for growing plants (known as a "GrowBot") and valued at $50,000 was stolen from a parking lot full of security guards at a marijuana trade show in Denver. It was pathetically easy to steal. During the end-of-the-show confusion, a Dodge truck pulled into the parking lot at the *High Times* Medical Cannabis Cup, hitched up the twenty-eight-foot grow trailer, and drove away. The twelve-foot-high, airtight GrowBot was filled with grow lights, an irrigation system, and mechanical shelves, and could be operated remotely by cell phone. When asked who he thought stole it, the owner replied, "Potheads—they're pretty stupid." But the real stupidity was that of the owner. What was he thinking? Not about security, obviously. There was a sign on the trailer indicating precisely what it was.

So, what do you do if thieves break into your yard or house and you catch them in the act of theft? Do not confront the thieves under any circumstances. If you are growing illegally, do not interfere and let them take what they want. You can always grow more plants—they're replaceable, but you're not. If you are growing legally, then you have a lot more options. First, call 911 and report a burglary in progress, then get out of the way. Be sure that you have all of your documentation available to show the authorities. Again, do not confront the thieves. You have nothing to gain and everything to lose, so let the police do what they are trained to do. Even if you have police or military training, stopping the thieves is not your job at this moment—getting assistance is what you need most.

If you come home and find the house breached and all your plants stolen (and possibly even your equipment), your entire growing operation has been compromised, perhaps permanently. No amount of home security can prevent a break-in if the thieves are determined and they have the right house-breaking equipment. Short of twenty-four-hour-a-day human security at your house, there is little you can do. But this scenario is unlikely, if you consider security to be number one on your planning checklist.

So, let's review your security planning checklist before we move on to planning your marijuana garden. First, pick the most logical place to grow your marijuana securely. Install the appropriate protective devices, ranging from simple locks and signs to high-tech options. Then settle into a lifestyle that appears as normal as possible, regardless of your previous lifestyle or current political beliefs. Finally, use whatever methods are necessary to camouflage your plants or your grow room. After taking all these steps, you should also be realistic and remember that your security can still be breached. I think good ole Benjamin Franklin said it best: "By failing to prepare, you are preparing to fail."

CHAPTER 3

Your Marijuana Oasis

Indoor, Outdoor, or Both

This chapter assumes that you have assessed possible growing locations based on the security protocols recommended in the previous chapter and you're ready for the next step, which is combining that information with the factors in this chapter to determine what your growing strategy will be. There are many options to choose from, and they vary in terms of expense, ease of growing, risk factors, and crop yield. By examining all of the possibilities for the location you've chosen, you will be able to decide which growing scenario works best for you.

Where to Grow?

There are three basic growing strategies you can use: outdoors, indoors, or both. Outdoor growing is by far the easier and less expensive route to take, and the benefits are faster growth, increased production, fewer plant pests to worry about, a smaller investment in equipment, and no electrical costs. The main drawback is an increased security risk because of the number and size of the plants you are trying to conceal. Another drawback is the fact that you will be at the mercy of the natural day-night cycle, and thus will be unable to trigger flowering by simulating the fall conditions of shorter days and longer nights. I think the key factor in determining if you should grow outdoors is your own unique yard situation. Do you have a high wall or fence that people cannot look over? Is there adequate concealing vegetation? Is there room for a structure of any kind that could hold your plants? If you answered yes to all three questions, outdoor growing is definitely a possibility.

Indoor growing requires an investment in building the proper grow room with sufficient lighting and ventilation, but you'll have much better security inside and out. But your yields will be much less; plant pests like spider mites, whiteflies, and mealybugs are more prevalent; and your electricity bill will be larger. Do you have a basement, crawl space, attic, or remote closet that you can use as a grow room? Can you devise adequate ventilation and air circulation? Can you afford to double your electricity costs? If you answered yes to all three of these questions, then indoor growing is a distinct possibility for you. If your location meets the requirements for both outdoor and indoor growing, as Leo's did, all the better, because that offers you more options. But first, let's look at the legal issues involved in deciding your growing strategy.

Legal Considerations for Growing

The number of plants you can grow legally varies by state, ranging from a low of six plants in Alaska, Colorado, and Maine to a high of eighteen in California and twenty-four in Oregon. Obviously, you should check the law in your state to make sure you are not exceeding the number allowed. Some states require that some of the plants be immature, meaning nonflowering, so check that as well. The immature plant requirement is actually a positive thing for growers because it forces them into a cycle of continuous production. Of course, continuous outdoor production ceases in the winter in most states where marijuana is legal to grow under state license, with the exception of southern Arizona, California, and all of Hawaii. In the other states, growers can use indoor facilities in winter and move the operation outdoors from approximately May through mid-October, assuming that their location is suitable for both scenarios.

In this chapter, I'm going to describe the process of planning a garden based on twelve plants, six mature and six immature. You can scale your garden upward or downward according to the law in your state. The restrictions about the number of plants are actually another good thing, because they counter the temptation to have garden overproduction. Remember, the more plants you have—especially flowering plants—the more valuable they will be and the greater target they will be. They will also be much more visible in an outdoor

garden. It's considerably easier to conceal six plants than twenty-four.

With moderate consumption habits and continuous production, the ideal number of plants to supply one person is approximately eight to twelve, depending on variety, yield, and consumption. This assumes, of course, that you put ample effort into both planning and growing. Keep in mind that the amount of harvested and dried marijuana you can possess ranges from one ounce in Alaska to twenty-four in Oregon and Washington, so it makes no sense to have a number of plants that can produce more marijuana than you can either use or possess. Another factor to consider is choosing the varieties that combine the traits of small size and good production—that is

Leo cannot grow this number of plants, but his friend in another state is allowed to.

discussed in chapter 4. A plant that reaches a maximum height of three feet is easier to control and conceal than one that grows eight feet tall. There is no officially documented "tallest marijuana plant" record, but some *sativa* varieties are known to reach twenty feet.

Factoring into your decision about growing indoors, outdoors, or both is the equipment you will need for your garden, so next we'll consider containers, "soil," fertilizers, lights—everything you need for growing outdoors.

LEO'S GROWING SOLUTION

Fortunately for him, Leo's property has a walled backyard with large, mature trees and shrubs, but still plenty of sunlight. It is secured with two locked gates, one on either side of the house, and it is difficult to look over the walls because of the bamboo and Virginia creeper vines planted along the walls. His house doesn't have an attic or basement, but it does have a secured garage, which he uses for art and craft projects; a crawl space with a ceiling height of about five feet; and a secured, locked office. Leo decided to start the seedlings indoors under small grow lights in his garage and office. When the plants were about a foot and a half tall, he moved them outdoors to his urban garden, a covered, raised bed (described in chapter 2). He also moved some of the plants to the crawl space, where he used stronger lighting and a fan for air circulation. This was an experiment that went somewhat awry, as we will see later. However, overall, his indoor/outdoor strategy was very successful.

Leo's simple setup: plants this size or even smaller are started indoors, then moved to his urban garden for vegetative growth, then moved back indoors for flowering under sodium lights.

Choosing the
Right Containers

To a certain extent your container selection will be determined by your garden location. For example, you won't be using five-gallon containers indoors because they'll take up too much room under the lights. In an indoor situation, one- or two-gallon pots are a better choice. Containers are essential for indoor growing, but I recommend them for outdoor cultivation as well because they're easy to move around and conceal as your other outdoor plants grow and mature. (If you don't have other outdoor plants, now is a good time to select and plant some as support for your marijuana garden.)

Although you can grow marijuana in any container that will hold soil and water, outdoors the best kind are the three- or five-gallon light plastic pots, the type that nurseries use for selling small trees and shrubs. Forget about pretty pots like decorated clay planters—they simply aren't needed and will be concealed anyway, unless you feel confident in showing off your garden or have no guests. You could always paint the pots green or camouflage, if you think that will conceal them better.

The most important thing to consider with containers is drainage. Marijuana plants do not like their roots to be constantly flooded with water. In the three-gallon pots, make sure there are sufficient drainage holes—in other words, more than a single small hole. If the holes are larger than a half inch in diameter, plug them with stones just slightly larger than the holes to prevent the soil from washing out. Gravity and porous soil will ensure good drainage no matter how much water you give them.

You can start your small plants in smaller pots, like ones with a six-inch diameter, and then transplant them to increasingly larger pots if you wish. Marijuana plants produce a lot of roots that can quickly fill pots. This constricts the roots and the plants become *root-bound*. So, as the roots fill a pot and start working their way out of the drainage holes, transplant them to larger pots.

The good news is that marijuana is a hardy plant that can adapt to constricted roots in small pots as long as it has sufficient water and nutrients. If you have the room, after the seedlings grow to the optimum size, with three or four sets of leaves, transplant them to the pots you will use—smaller ones for indoors and three- to five-gallon pots for outdoors—and leave them there, saving yourself all the extra work of constantly repotting. While growers constantly debate the subject of constricted roots, I suggest you use the largest pots possible for your growing situation, whether it's indoors or outdoors. I have seen vigorous and healthy flowering marijuana plants six feet tall in three-gallon containers, so that's proof in itself that the plant is happy despite somewhat constricted roots. Leo adds that if you're concerned about root constriction, use five-gallon pots if you have the room. The extra cost is minimal and watering frequency diminishes.

Selecting the "Soil"

The selection of the growing medium for your plants is critical for maximum plant performance, especially indoors because of the artificial environment you are creating. The growing medium provides support for the stems and foliage, and delivers water, air, and nutrients to the roots, so you don't want to take chances or cut corners when selecting one.

The term "soil" is a bit of a misnomer for the marijuana gardener, because you should never use soil from your garden in containers. It will be much too dense and will compact (this is called "caking") and not allow the roots to grow properly. In fact, most potting soils that you buy at a garden center or nursery have no real soil in them at all, and that's why I use the term "growing medium."

In the garden, soil is a combination of air, water, rock particles, mineral salts, organic material (humus), and living organisms including bacteria, fungi, algae, protozoa, worms, and various insects. Of course, marijuana will grow quite well in garden soil as long as it's not confined in containers. However, you should add organic material from your compost pile before you plant—more composting suggestions are in chapter 6. If you don't have a compost pile, I will tell you how to make one, or you can just buy sterilized steer manure in bags at your garden center. You can add *perlite* (amorphous volcanic glass) to the outdoor garden soil for drainage and soil aeration, and the roots will grow faster—more on this subject in chapter 6.

For years, I mixed my own growing medium based on the formula I learned from my father. But these days such attention to detail is not necessary because marijuana will grow well in most commercial potting soil like Miracle-Gro or knockoffs with a similar composition, which is usually sphagnum peat moss, perlite, and time-release fertilizer. That's it. (You can find this potting soil at the big box stores.) My grower friends turn up their noses at such common growing media and prefer FoxFarm Ocean Forest, which is composed of peat moss, with "forest humus," fish and crab meal, shrimp meal, bat guano, and earthworm castings. It's true that marijuana grows well in this medium, with one caveat: it costs a little over $8 a cubic foot, while Miracle-Gro and other brands is more than a dollar less per cubic foot. In my opinion, either medium works fine as long as you realize that marijuana will exhaust the built-in fertilizer in a few weeks and you will need to add more fertilizer as the plants grow larger—this, too, I discuss in detail later in chapter 6.

Some growers insist that your container soil can only be used for one season and then it should be thrown away or mixed into the garden soil (for either marijuana or crops like tomatoes or peppers) in order to loosen it up. This is not necessarily true. You can save some money by recycling the container soil you use by following this three-step method.

1. Leach out any remaining fertilizers from pots used the previous year. Just keep running water through the pot until the water runs clear.

2. Mix the old soil with newly purchased soil one-to-one, while adding perlite in the ratio of one cup to two gallons of potting soil.

3. Sterilize this new soil by solarizing it and letting ultraviolet light do the work. In the sunniest part of your yard, put down a sheet of black plastic. Spread a thin layer of the new soil mix over the plastic. Cover this with a sheet of clear plastic and weigh down the edges with bricks or rocks. Two days in the sun is enough to sterilize the soil and turn it into a productive growing medium with one addition: fertilizer.

Fertilizers and Marijuana's Nutrient Needs

Fertilizers are any organic or inorganic substances that provide the nutrients necessary for plant growth. They usually combine the *macronutrients* (the ones plants use the most) with *micronutrients*, or trace elements, that plants need for specific purposes. Besides carbon, hydrogen, and oxygen, which all plants need, the three most-needed macronutrients for marijuana are nitrogen, phosphorous, and potassium, indicated on fertilizer labels by their chemical designations: N, P, and K.

Plants differ in their nutrient needs, but basically marijuana needs nitrogen for vegetative growth (stems and leaves), phosphorous for plant vigor and flowering, and potassium for good flowering, which is the ultimate goal of the marijuana grower. Therefore, more nitrogen is needed during the early growth stages and more phosphorous and potassium are required during the flowering period. To deliver the nutrients in the best possible way, two types of fertilizers are recommended: timed-release fertilizers in granular form that are mixed into the soil, and water-soluble fertilizers that are mixed with the water used for watering the plants. Both are suitable for containers and outdoor gardens, but I recommend the water-soluble fertilizers because you can adjust the nutrient levels better for vegetative growth and then flowering.

Back when I was growing marijuana, I used weak solutions of Peters or Miracle-Gro 20-20-20 (N, P, K) water-soluble fertilizer (the bright blue stuff), and they worked fine for me. Leo, of course, chimes in with, "Friends don't let friends use Miracle-Gro," but that's just Leo. He and a lot of other growers believe that organic fertilizers are superior to inorganic ones despite the lack of scientific evidence that this is true. Plant scientists at New Mexico State University, where I am a member of the adjunct faculty, have told me that, for example, as long as nitrogen is provided for the plant, it does not care whether the source is organic or synthetic.

Now you can choose from a myriad of fertilizers, some designed for vegetative growth and some for flowering. The growers I know prefer FoxFarm organic fertilizers,

Some growers disdain "common" growing media and prefer the FoxFarm Ocean Forest shown here.

This grow room is about as packed as possible, proving that you can grow a lot of cannabis in cramped circumstances.

including premixed Tiger Bloom. Compare that to synthetic Miracle-Gro LiquaFeed Bloom Booster Flower Food, which is about half the cost. The decision to use organic or synthetic fertilizers is a personal matter that sometimes comes down to individual belief systems. As with religion and politics, there are true believers in the garden world who fervently swear by organic-only techniques, but I agree with the plant scientists that the plant doesn't really care as long as it receives the proper nutrients. This thinking is considered heresy by die-hard organic gardeners, like tree-hugger Leo, who says, without any empirical evidence, "If it's organic, it's orgasmic—you can't fake it." Whichever you prefer, using a high-nitrogen fertilizer for vegetative growth and a high-phosphorous fertilizer when blooming begins

will produce more flowers and could possibly increase the amount of THC in those flowers. Leo believes that marijuana's THC level is determined only by a plant's genetics, but that's not true with the capsaicin in chile peppers, where environment plays up to a 50 percent role in the heat level of the pods. (For example, stressing chile pepper plants by withholding water until they wilt slightly can increase heat levels in the pods.)

Stress can definitely affect marijuana plants. Botanists have noted several types of stress plants can experience, such as near-freezing temperatures, nutrient excess or deficiency, physical mutilation, or light-cycle changes. Such stress can alter the usual one-to-one ratio of male to female plants, diminish seed production, interfere with disease

YOU LUCKY GREENHOUSE GROWER, YOU . . . : OR NOT

I've maintained a small greenhouse for most of my adult life—a necessity because I'm a food and garden writer who's constantly experimenting with new plants other than marijuana. I need to germinate chile and tomato seeds in the spring. I also love tropical and subtropical plants like bananas, hibiscus, mangos, and Meyer lemons, so I need a greenhouse to winter them over.

But a winter greenhouse is not the ideal place to grow marijuana. Winter light is not the best light for growing marijuana. Not only are the days shorter, which provides less total light for the plant, but also the intensity of light in the northern hemisphere is greatly reduced because of the low angle of the sun. Some sources indicate that winter light intensity is often less than one-tenth of that of typical summer daylight, which greatly inhibits plant growth because it reduces photosynthesis. In simple terms, plants that require intense light cannot produce enough food for themselves during the low light of winter, causing leaf

yellowing and dropping. Essentially they are dropping inefficient leaves and making new ones closer to the light source at the top of plants. And the leaves are usually narrower and more delicate, further reducing their effectiveness and causing the plants to become "leggy."

Marijuana is demanding of full sunlight, and if it doesn't get it, its quality diminishes. A high level of THC requires intense light, and the low light in a winter greenhouse will make a high level difficult, if not impossible, to achieve. In other words, the potency of marijuana grown under winter low-light conditions is significantly reduced. Adding lights to correct this requires a waterproof greenhouse roof. In addition, insect pests are always a problem in the winter greenhouse.

Some growers attempt to use a sunroom for marijuana cultivation, but I don't think that they're efficient at all. In the summer, the sun is too high in the sky, so the angle is wrong for most sunrooms and the plants will receive diffused light rather than direct light. In winter, the sun is lower, so the plants will receive direct light, but it's not strong enough for proper growth, just as in the greenhouse. I say forget about using a greenhouse or sunroom and simply grow the plants under HID lamps.

Growing marijuana in a greenhouse like this one—where Mario Dadomo grows chile peppers at the Azienda Agraria Sperimentale Stuard in Parma, Italy—would be overkill for a medical marijuana operation. But one can always fantasize.

resistance in clones, produce *hermaphroditic plants* (plants with both male and female structures), and alter the *phenotype* (growing habit) of the plants.

Building the Indoor Grow Room

I'm going to start with the equipment and environment needed for an indoor marijuana garden and then later discuss growing techniques. The medical marijuana grower with a mere twelve plants is hardly creating a marijuana-growing factory, so much of what you may have heard or read about how expensive it is to grow marijuana indoors has been exaggerated and simply does not apply to your situation. Mylar on the walls to maximize reflection? Unnecessary. Large exhaust fans? Not needed. Banks of lights with huge ballasts that require special wiring? Overkill. Here's how to do it on a budget.

Choosing the room to use for growing involves numerous factors beyond just security. A properly rigged closet (see illustration, page 49) can be used, as well as a spare bedroom, but I like attics or basements because they are far less accessible. Guests looking for the bathroom may open a door by mistake, but they're not going into your attic or basement without an invitation. Whichever room you choose should have some ventilation that doesn't leak light, like a vent with a small, quiet exhaust fan, an adequate source of electricity, and systems that prevent water leakage, especially in attics.

Choosing Lighting

As to the types of lights you need to grow marijuana, there are at least forty-seven different bulbs ranging from 250 to 1,000 watts. So how do you choose which lighting system to use? Instead of focusing first on the bulbs, let's take a look at the different types of lights and my recommendations:

- Incandescent home lighting: not recommended because it's not bright enough and it doesn't generate a lot of heat.

- Fluorescent, office-style light tubes: an inexpensive solution that I used for years, but not the best option because they do not have the proper light spectrum for growing plants.

- Halogen lights: these get too hot and are not recommended.

- High-intensity discharge lights (HID): these are the best lighting systems to use and they include metal halide, high-pressure sodium, and mercury-vapor lights. These days, mercury-vapor lights are uncommon because they are not sold by indoor-growing retailers, so most growers use either metal halide or high-pressure sodium lighting systems, or both, which I discuss below.

A *metal-halide light* produces light by an electric arc through a gaseous mixture of vaporized mercury and *metal halides* (a combination of a metal and a halogen such as chlorine). A *high-pressure sodium lamp* is similar but uses gaseous sodium instead of mercury (that's the "metal") halide gas. Both systems have two basic parts: a ballast that provides the power and a lamp that emits the light. Some experts say that metal-halide lights are best for vegetative growing but recommend switching to high-pressure sodium systems for flowering. But buying two completely different systems is expensive, so I recommend a logical solution: buy a metal-halide system, complete with a bulb, and then buy a conversion bulb that provides the spectrum of high-pressure sodium for flowering but runs off the same ballast as a metal-halide bulb. The conversion bulb provides an orange-red spectrum, which is ideal for flowering because it produces the densest flowers, increasing the yield. That said, you can use a high-pressure sodium unit for the entire growth cycle, but the lamps lack the blue spectrum, and the plants can stretch too much toward the light, making the plants "leggy" instead of bushy, which is what you ideally want the plants to be.

The parts of a metal-halide growing system are simple: a bulb, a reflector hood that houses the bulb, the ballast that provides the necessary power, and a power cord. Add-on features include air-cooling flanges designed to cool the heat generated by the bulb, a small cooling fan for bulbs with a higher wattage that produce more heat, and larger horizontal reflectors to better spread the light. Generally speaking, a metal-halide system that's 400 watts with a standard horizontal reflector will cover 9 square feet, or 3 feet by 3 feet, while a 600-watt system will cover a little over 12 square feet (3½ by 3½ feet).

Light operates under the inverse square law, which means that light strength is inversely proportional to the square of the distance from the source of the light. Simply put, if you double the distance between the light source and the plants, each plant will receive one-fourth the light it was previously receiving. Thus, plants should be as close to the light source as possible without burning them with the heat. So you should always have a fan in the grow room to circulate the air and prevent the heat from building up near the plants.

Preparing a Hidden Closet Grow Space

For growers who cannot devote a room or even part of a basement or attic to their indoor marijuana garden, the use of a closet is a definite possibility. But if you take this direction, you will first have to modify the closet to create proper venting and air circulation, as well as install electric power strips, and you'll have to do the work yourself—or have a close friend or relative do it. You would not want to hire a contractor because the project would be suspicious—why would anyone want to ventilate a closet to the outside except to grow or cook something?

To prepare your grow closet:

- Use a closet in a part of your house where guests will not go—ideally abutting an exterior wall.

- Install a discreet lock on the door.

- Paint the walls with a high-gloss white paint, which will aid with light reflection and cleanup, because inside growing involving soil, water, and fertilizer is messy and you want to keep the closet as clean as possible.

- On the bottom of the door, attach an insulation strip painted the same color as the door—this will seal the closet and prevent light and odors from escaping.

- Install adjustable shelving so that plants of different heights will all be the same distance from the lights. Ideally, you should have both adjustable shelves and adjustable lights.

- Attach the lights to the ceiling of the closet with small chains that can be raised or lowered. The adjustability of the system will keep the lights the proper distance from the plants as they grow.

- Cut an air intake hole at the bottom of the closet wall. You'll want to disguise it in some way, depending on how the closet is situated in the house. Use a standard heating vent cover identical to the ones already in your house and no one will notice it.

- At the top of the closet, you'll have to engineer a vent hole to the outside with an exhaust fan built into it. Just think about the way clothes dryers are vented— it's the same principle with a small exhaust fan added. Yes, heated air rises, but in the confines of a closet, it might not rise fast enough to adequately circulate around the plants. This venting will require you to breach an exterior wall, and you don't want an obvious hole in your house, so place a vent cover over the hole, one with flaps that respond to the air pressure from the fan. You can use metal tubing or even a dryer hose to connect the covered hole to the inside of the closet. Remember to paint the vent cover the same color as the outside of the house.

You could divide the closet into upper and lower chambers, one for vegetative growth and one for flowering, but since you would have to open the door to water and care for the plants, the day/night cycle for flowering will be interrupted. It's better just to switch out the bulb for flowering, but use the same ballast and reflector.

Leo considered using the closet option after he first learned about 'Lowryder #2', a short variety that would be a perfect candidate for a closet grow room. But since he has other growing locations in and around his house, he decided not to limit his operation to one variety. He said that the closet option would be better for town house owners, who often have no yards to speak of, and neither a basement nor an attic. For other varieties suitable for closet growing, see chapter 4.

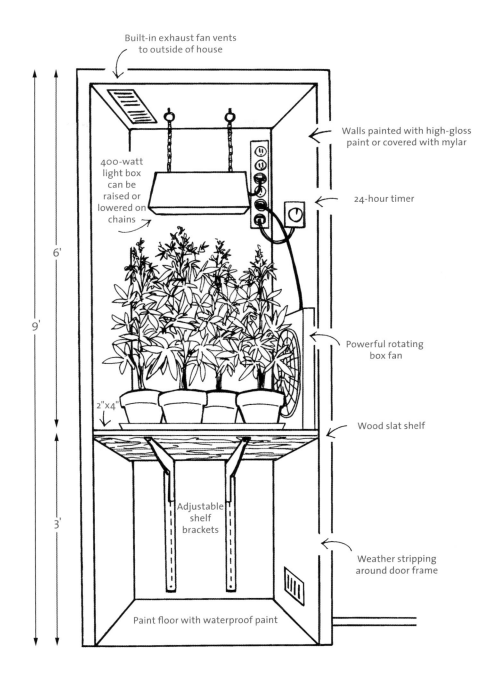

Built-in exhaust fan vents to outside of house

Walls painted with high-gloss paint or covered with mylar

400-watt light box can be raised or lowered on chains

24-hour timer

Powerful rotating box fan

2"x4"

Wood slat shelf

Adjustable shelf brackets

Weather stripping around door frame

Paint floor with waterproof paint

9'

6'

3'

A typical schematic for a grow closet.

HYDROPONICS OR NOT?

I do not recommend hydroponics for small-scale medical marijuana growing. This is not to imply that there's something inherently wrong with that method of growing, but it doesn't fit the theme of this book, which is growing marijuana quickly and easily. Hydroponics can produce the plants just as quickly as "soil gardening," but easy it's not.

Supporters of hydroponics make a good case for their method. It uses much less water, it's easier to control the application of nutrients, it's more efficient, and in some ways, less messy. They claim higher crop yields, quicker plant maturation, reduced problems with soil-borne pests, and more overall control of the plants' environment. All of this may be true, but for growing a mere twelve plants? The critics of hydroponic marijuana gardening point out that hydroponic systems are much more expensive than plastic pots filled with a growing medium, they are complicated so the learning curve for using them is high, and growers must acquire more skills to operate the systems efficiently. There's also the pesky problem of water-borne plant diseases that can spread quickly to the entire system.

Clearly, this method is best for large-scale, clandestine growing operations, and not for the growing of medical marijuana for personal use. Hydroponic systems have high maintenance requirements and more things that can

Yes, you can grow marijuana hydroponically, but why bother for a small garden of medical marijuana?

go wrong. Until marijuana is completely legal in your state, with no limitations on the amount you can grow, don't bother with it. If you become a dedicated grower and want to give it a try, think of hydroponics as the next step in your growing operation, a "phase two," so to speak.

Indoor growing in a much larger space, such as a garage or attic that is not readily accessible, is easier than in a closet because remodeling is not necessary. However, there are some precautions to take. If you have a grow room with lights on a timer, make sure that there are no light leaks that would signal to a neighbor that something odd is going on at your house. Most of the lights you would be using are much brighter than normal lighting, so you don't want such brightness leaking out from cracks. Use duct tape or foam weather stripping to seal light leaks, and test your system by turning off all the lights in the house except for those in the grow room. Allow time for your eyes to adjust to the darkness and if you see any leaks, seal them thoroughly.

Creating an Outdoor Marijuana Oasis

When it comes to designing an outdoor marijuana garden, the biggest consideration is how to hide your plants from prying eyes. Think about how it might appear to visitors on the ground or even from the air. Who are you allowing into your backyard, if anyone? What would your garden look like to a low-hovering helicopter? Even if you are growing legally, you don't want to be obvious about it. The state police in a helicopter won't necessarily know you're growing legally and might investigate or count your plants and pay you a visit. And then even more people will know about your garden. Since it's still a federal crime to grow this plant, your overall strategy must

fully utilize all the techniques of concealment and the integration of marijuana into your vegetable and flower gardens, if you have them. If not, you may have to become a more general gardener, which is not difficult at all. If you don't care about growing anything other than marijuana, I suggest selecting an indoor option.

I discussed marijuana lookalikes and plants to screen off your outdoor growing in chapter 2, but in the planning stage you're in now, I'm going to suggest an additional strategy—that of weaving your marijuana plants into your existing or soon-to-be vegetable and flower gardens. Marijuana will fit into either of them with a little attention to detail. The biggest challenge you'll have is when the large marijuana varieties grow too much to be easily

Marijuana can be trained to grow along a trellis interspersed with other trellis-loving plants.

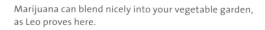

Marijuana can blend nicely into your vegetable garden, as Leo proves here.

concealed. Either you have to prune them severely and turn them into a small bush, or use creative techniques like trellising to further disguise their appearance. If you grow grapes on trellises, for example, a few trellised marijuana plants would fit in fine, either planted in the ground or in pots. You can always bury the pots in the soil to further disguise them. In the trellising scenario, all you have to do is dig a hole next to the trellis, place a pot full of growing medium in it, and then transplant the marijuana seedlings into the pot. The marijuana leaves would be obscured by the grape (or other plant) leaves and the pots would be invisible. A far better solution is to use only small varieties outside; some preferred ones are listed in chapter 4.

If the varieties you select are small or medium size, they would fit well into a tomato garden. Tomatoes that are placed in cages of metal wire to keep the plants from sprawling or collapsing from the *fruit load* (a whole bunch of tomatoes on an unsupported plant) grow tall and wide and are good companion plants as they hide marijuana reasonably well. The

only chile peppers that would work as well as tomatoes for this purpose are some varieties in the *baccatum* species that resemble small trees—like 'Ají Amarillo'. As mentioned in chapter 2, corn or maize works well for inter-cropping, but both corn and marijuana are nutrient consumers—they love nitrogen—so if you grow them together, you will have to apply more fertilizer than usual.

Flower gardeners will find more companion plant possibilities than vegetable gardeners. I mentioned *Vitex*, the plant with compound palmate leaves and a similar bloom stalk that is white when immature but bright purple when mature. Other densely standing, heavily flowering varieties that would work as companion plants or screening plants include Maximilian daisy (*Helianthus maximilianii*), silver lace vine (*Fallopia baldschuanica*), goldenrod (*Solidago canadensis*) and some varieties of *Penstemon*, *Salvia*, *Lavandula*, *Agastache*, *Baptisia*, and *Monarda*. The eyes of the casual visitors to your oasis will be drawn to the tops of the plants, to the bright flowers, and they will not see other foliage concealed beneath the blooms.

If you are one of the fortunate gardeners with the will and the funds to design your own marijuana garden, you can cleverly hide your plants with elevated, bricked beds two feet high and three feet wide that are in front of an eight-foot-tall wall or fence. The front of the bed would have groundcover and low-blooming plants, the center would have tall plants as a screen, and your favorite crop would be hidden behind the dense foliage screen. The tall, raised bed is a physical barrier that further isolates the marijuana plants from prying eyes.

Another clever technique is using actual arbors or screens—decorative garden screens, that is. Who knows what's behind a densely planted rose trellis? Or an intricate, manufactured screen made from bamboo? A typical Japanese screen would look nice next to a green-leafed Japanese maple with its compound, palmate leaves. "It is permissible to have fun with your oasis," says Leo.

Raised beds without covers.

Raised Bed Marijuana Gardens

I've grown all kinds of plants in various types of gardens, from rows and furrows to flat beds to modified irrigated beds, but my favorite design by far is the raised bed because it's a gardening control freak's dream come true. "Leave nothing to chance" is my mantra, and although that goal is very difficult to achieve, a raised-bed system comes closer to it than any previous one I've used.

First, the soil here in the Southwest, where I live, is alkaline and often so packed that it forms a nearly impenetrable deposit in the soil called *caliche*, which is a hardened deposit of calcium carbonate that has cemented all the soil particles together. I use the term "cement" accurately because caliche is used to make actual cement in west Texas. A raised bed allows you to avoid such excessive alkalinity because you can perfect the recipe for your own soil mix—just think of your raised bed as a very, very large container. And in the parts of the country where gophers are a problem, gopher wire at the bottom of the raised bed can keep the gophers from having their own pot party.

I built my raised bed with four two-by-eight boards. I simply nailed the boards together and set them in the garden. Then I removed about four inches of garden soil from the bed to get it ready for the new soil. I don't use any soil from my backyard in my recipe, although it will be there, a foot below the soil that I have created by using packaged "top soil" sold at big box home stores. Ingredients in these soils, which are sometimes labeled as "organic," include composted plant and wood products (such as peat or sphagnum peat), lava sand and silt, sandy loam, gypsum, and sometimes urea to add a little nitrogen to the mix. The cost is reasonable, just a few dollars per cubic foot.

I completely fill my two raised beds, add my two-year-old compost until it's about 20 percent of the entire mixture, and then I rototill it together and test the drainage by flooding the beds with the garden hose. If the water stands for more than thirty seconds (that's never happened, but it could), I would add perlite in fairly large amounts. Most of the time the water drains completely in seconds, and that's excellent drainage.

Irrigating the Beds

The next step is irrigation. Forget about installing drip lines—they are expensive and easily damaged, and they clog up, especially due to the salts accumulating from alkaline water. Use soaker hoses, also known as weeper hoses and drip hoses, but not the round ones made from recycled tires. They burst easily if the water pressure is high, have uneven application of water, and cannot hold up to

ultraviolet radiation. Use the flat hoses made from nylon—I like Gilmour hoses because they are seemingly indestructible and provide a very even and steady drip. In a single bed four feet wide, I place three parallel lines of soaker hoses, and depending on rainfall, I water twice a week by leaving the soakers on for about an hour.

Adding Mulch

Next comes the first layer of mulch: landscape fabric over the soaker hoses. *Landscape fabrics*, also called geotextiles, are usually made from a synthetic like polypropylene and can be perforated, woven, or spun-bonded. Unlike row covers, made from similar materials and sold in different colors, landscape fabrics are usually black. They help with weed control and permit the movement of air and water from rainfall into the soil, so they are much better than black plastic sheeting. I especially like landscape fabric because it helps keep the soil warm in the early spring. I use a staple gun to tack the fabric to the wood frame of the bed. There are, as usual, some whiners and moaners on Internet garden forums that don't like the stuff. "I used it and had weeds coming through it!" wrote one horrified and probably inexperienced gardener. Although some groundcover weeds will occasionally penetrate the fabric, or more likely germinate in the detritus on top of the fabric, it is excellent for weed control, especially when a second layer of mulch is applied. And that second layer would be untreated landscaping bark, which is excellent for creating an organic barrier against

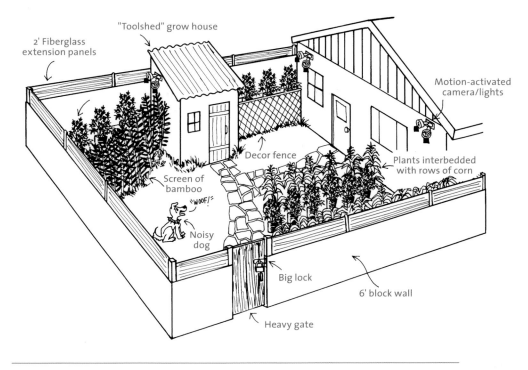

Labels on illustration:
- 2' Fiberglass extension panels
- "Toolshed" grow house
- Motion-activated camera/lights
- Decor fence
- Plants interbedded with rows of corn
- Screen of bamboo
- *WOOF!*
- Noisy dog
- Big lock
- 6' block wall
- Heavy gate

Growing in a backyard garden requires special measures to protect the crop from prying neighbors.

evaporation from the soil through the fabric. This mulch can be reused every year, but the fabric must be replaced annually.

After the fabric is tacked down, marijuana growers can plant their seedlings (see chapter 5). Use a trowel to cut through the fabric and then scoop out a hole and place the scooped-out soil on a sheet of newspaper. Add whatever soil amendments and fertilizer you intend to use at this time. Place the small plants in the hole, replace the dirt, and proceed to add the second layer of mulch (the bark) after all the bedding plants are in place.

Of course, there is a huge debate about using the same soil mix in the raised bed every year, and I've been chastised for that. However, by adding compost every spring (see chapter 6),

I rejuvenate the soil and continue to have a bountiful garden. If I see anything wrong with the plants or the yield, I will dig out half of the soil and use it to dress the ornamental plants in my other raised beds.

Now that you've incorporated the security requirements with your own personal growing scenarios and planned your strategy, it's time to select the varieties you will grow.

CHAPTER 4

Blueberry or Lemon?

Recommended Varieties

It was the early 1970s; I still lived in the South and worked as a production director of an "underground" radio station, and I had written and produced the national radio commercial for the rerelease of *Reefer Madness*, the 1930s ridiculous (and hilarious to watch when stoned) movie that swept college towns for midnight showings. Around this time, Commander Cody and His Lost Planet Airmen were lamenting in song, "I'm down to seeds and stems again," which was not exactly the position I was in. I had plenty of seeds, sure, and I was putting them to good use rather than trying to smoke them (not recommended) or throwing them out like everyone else was doing. They were undoubtedly some common, unnamed Mexican *sativa* variety, not the high-quality 'Acapulco Gold' or 'Red Hair.' While others were pitching their seeds in someone else's trash can, I was sprouting them for my basement grow room. They had no cash value and no other use. I knew about growing *sinsemilla*, but that was the extent of my "advanced" growing knowledge. Things are much different in today's world of marijuana cultivation because growers have so many varieties to choose from. Leo and I have chosen the varieties that follow as a starting point for the first-time grower.

Acquiring Seed

Today seeds of 'Acapulco Gold' or 'Red Hair' have no value, but more important, no grower wants to use them. Rather, the home medical marijuana cultivator would rather pay for specialty seeds that have been bred specifically for certain traits. Leo, for example, decided to use the services of a company in the United Kingdom that is part of a vast network of underground amateur marijuana breeders who had developed, according to one source, several thousand marijuana "strains." But some are simple F1 hybrids (a first-generation cross between two established varieties) and not true varieties because they will not produce plants with uniform characteristics. The analogy of dogs works perfectly here: When you cross a cocker spaniel with a poodle, you get a mutt. It would take many more generations of selective breeding before you developed a cockapoo breed.

When was the last time that amateur breeders conquered a specific plant and triumphed over professional botanists and horticulturists? I think it was the rose breeders, and the amateur marijuana breeders have followed their path despite the fact that roses are perfectly legal while marijuana, of course, is still entrapped in a murky quagmire of legality, especially in the United States. And all this confusion begins with the seeds.

Marijuana seeds can be free or quite expensive, depending on the success of your growing project.

The Bad Seed (with Some Good News)

Marijuana seeds contain no THC, yet it is still illegal to possess them in the United States, except if you live in a state that allows cultivation. Maybe. About half of the seventeen states that allow medical marijuana require individual patients or their caregivers to grow their own plants. But many of those states do not have a policy regarding how those growers should acquire the seeds or seedlings to start growing. For example, in New Mexico, until recently, medical marijuana patients who were authorized to grow their own marijuana didn't have any legal ways to buy seeds or starter plants except from a few dispensaries that were selling clones. But the dispensaries didn't sell seeds and they don't grow seed crops. The most commonly asked question is, "How do I get started? How do I get seeds?"

The answer, of course, is not what anyone wants to hear. Marijuana growers have no option but to use illegal methods to obtain the seeds they need to grow it legally. That's

the bad news. The good news is that there's very little risk in doing so. After an exhaustive search of online resources, I cannot find one instance where anyone has been arrested for ordering marijuana seeds from foreign (meaning non-US) suppliers. If, for example, the package containing the seeds is intercepted by the US Postal Service or the DEA, the seeds are confiscated and replaced with a stern note explaining the confiscation, and the package is sealed and sent on its way. Even the federal government doesn't want any part of that particular segment of the quagmire.

Obtaining Seeds

First, a disclaimer. I'm going to tell you how Leo got his seeds, and as usual, this information is purely historical and informational in nature and is not a guide to committing illegal acts. Leo's college training made him an excellent researcher, so he began a search for marijuana seed banks. In the semiunderground world of European marijuana, there are marijuana breeders who sell the seeds of their own varieties and thus become marijuana seed companies. (A selection of seed companies are listed in Resources.) Not only do they sell to the general public, they supply companies called marijuana seed banks. The seed banks usually are not the breeders and usually do not have their own varieties—they are merely retailers providing a broad spectrum of the most popular marijuana "strains." Green Man's Seedbank Update (seedbankupdate.com) is a handy online guide to seed banks. Online since 1998,

it describes itself this way: "Here you will find a list of honest seed banks with ratings based on reports from buyers of cannabis seeds."

The Attitude Seed Bank (cannabis-seeds-bank.co.uk) is the seed bank that Leo chose, for a number of important reasons. The first was communication. If a bank or seed company will promptly answer email questions, they're offering a great start to a business relationship. Second, they had a wide selection of varieties, an astonishing two thousand, so it was one-stop shopping instead of going through the same process over and over with a number of seed companies or banks. Third, they offered "Rapid Discreet Delivery Options" (what Leo calls "stealth shipping"), which means the seeds are concealed discreetly within a T-shirt, wallet, coffee mug, or CD and that is what's

A typical listing from the Attitude Seed Bank, complete with a photo and detailed description of the variety.

written on the customs declaration. And finally, Attitude promised—and delivered—prompt shipping. The seeds arrived quickly with no problems, had 100 percent germination (very remarkable), and Leo really likes his new wallet (made in China).

New Advances in Cannabis Breeding

In order to select the varieties for your medical marijuana garden, you should know something about the new varieties that have been developed not only to increase yields and their amount of THC, but also to better facilitate growing them indoors under lights.

Autoflower Power

Autoflowering varieties begin as essentially *ruderalis* plants hybridized with *indica* or *sativa* or both, and their flowering is triggered not by shorter days but by maturity—the plant goes directly from the immature stage to the flowering stage, skipping most of the usual vegetative growth. The original autoflowering strain, 'Lowryder', was created by the Joint Doctor and Highbred Seeds by back-breeding 'Northern Lights' and 'William's Wonder' with a Mexican *ruderalis*. It seems that the only *ruderalis* traits left in the hybrid are its low height and the autoflowering gene.

The life cycle of 'Lowryder' and varieties developed from it, like 'Lowryder #2', is short—less than three months. After sprouting, male plants start to develop their pollen sacs and the plants should be removed. About a week later,

the females start to bloom very quickly. When grown inside under lights (18 hours on, 6 hours off), they develop a single flowering top that usually weighs less than $1/2$ ounce when dried. However, if grown outside in a four-gallon pot under full sun, the plant will branch and more tops will develop, possibly doubling or tripling the yield. Light intensity, pot size, and fertilizer all play an important role in determining the size of your autoflowering marijuana plants at maturity, but the standard rule is this: the better the conditions, the bigger the yield. Because of the variety's quick development, cloning is impractical, so it is grown from seed only. But autoflowering varieties are ideal for staggered planting—one will always be

A 26-inch-tall 'Lowryder #2' in full flowering mode and very bushy. This autoflowering variety is perfect for small, contained gardens both inside and out.

blooming and you'll have a fresh harvest every few weeks.

Leo has grown some autoflowering varieties, including 'Lowryder #2', and the results have been successful. I sampled 'Lowryder #2' and the effect is excellent, and the *ruderalis* genes do not seem to have affected its potency. If you ever grow under lights in the limited space of a closet, autoflowering plants like 'Lowryder' and 'Lowryder #2' are the ones you should choose because they are small and mature quickly. Another good choice, according to Leo, is 'Diesel Ryder', a cross between 'New York City Diesel' and 'Lowryder #2'. However, remember that each little plant counts in your state-mandated plant count, so you will have to decide whether size or yield is more important.

You're So . . . Feminine

Marijuana growers typically waste a lot of time, energy, and money removing the male plants from their garden in order to grow *sinsemilla*, which are all-female plants whose flowers are not pollinated. But what if every seed you planted turned out to be female instead of the typical 50-50 ratio? You would get a head start with less work.

When an online seed company has a web page with a gorgeous topless woman almost covering her nipples with marijuana leaves and directly below is the comment "Feminized marijuana seeds represent the peak in quality and genetics of marijuana seeds," the BS sensors start ringing in my brain. Naturally the reason so many seed companies and banks are

A hermaphroditic top showing both male and female flowers.

pushing them is because they can make more money with them. There is no known method for treating existing normal seeds to feminize them, but you can create your own feminized seeds for the next growing cycle.

The basics behind creating all-female seeds are simple. A female flowering plant is induced to grow male pollen sacs and produce pollen. This pollen, which has only female genetic material, is used to fertilize other females. The results are seeds that will be mostly female. The seed companies would have you believe that the plants grown from these seeds are universally female. That's not always true, but at least with feminized seeds, the odds are a lot better than 50-50 for producing female plants.

There are several different ways to make the female plants produce male pollen sacs. Some females will do it as a result of stress from heat, while some will make a desperate attempt (forgive my anthropomorphism) to pollinate themselves because there are no males handy. There are two chemical treatments that will induce male parts on female plants: colloidal silver and gibberellic acid. But before you go to all that trouble, let's get another opinion.

Some seed companies don't sell feminized seeds and instead recommend cloning your female plants. One company calls feminized seeds an "unstable and unpredictable hermaphroditic breed." That said, at least 250 varieties of marijuana are available with seeds that are both feminized and autoflowering. Most feminized and autoflowering seeds are at least twice as expensive as regular seeds. From what I've read and experienced, making clones is, indeed, the answer for increasing the number of female plants if you're on a budget (more on this in chapter 7).

Seed Storage

If you are careful with the storage of your expensive foreign seeds, they will last a long time. Cannabis seeds are very similar in *viability* (capable of germination)—they are at their best the year after they are produced, but every year after that they take longer to sprout and the germination percentage declines. If

you plan to plant them within two years from the time you receive or grow them, they will be fine with just a few adjustments to their storage environment. Plastic film canisters—relics of the ancient past in the digital era—make great seed storage containers. Leo—a pack rat—has dozens of canisters and he says that they are readily available at drugstores like Walgreens. If you can't find any, use prescription medicine containers. Put the seeds in the canister, add a silica gel desiccant to remove any possible moisture, label the canisters with the variety name and date, put them in a box, and store it in the back of the lowest shelf of the refrigerator. Tell your spouse that they're crucial to your health.

If you intend to keep the seeds longer than a year or two, move the box with the canisters to the freezer. This is homemade cryogenics—

Marijuana seeds in a film canister headed to the freezer for long-term storage.

the temperature won't be minus 238°F, but it will preserve your seeds for years. Let's hope you don't need to save them that long and you are able to get them sprouting as soon as possible.

Choosing Your Marijuana Varieties

Matching appropriate varieties to your particular growing environment is crucial to the success of your marijuana garden. Some varieties will grow too large for growing under lights. Some will be too smelly for indoor growing, and some simply will not flourish under lights.

With thousands of marijuana varieties available and hundreds of growing scenarios, it is impossible to give descriptions of all the most popular and easy-to-grow varieties. So I've used Leo's first-year growing experiences in a typical home-growing setup as a model to choose some varieties that I think you'll have success growing. When choosing which varieties to recommend here, I used the following criteria to narrow down my list. Each recommended plant must have the ability to be

- started indoors under lights;

- grown to flowering outdoors (and disguised in a secure backyard);

- grown to flowering indoors under lights; and

- dried and cured indoors.

To meet these criteria, the varieties must also have the following characteristics.

- Size: not overly large at maturity

- Aroma of the flowering tops: mild (not too stinky)

- Amounts of THC and cannibidol (CBD) in the flowering tops: high (see sidebar, page 64)

- Length of time from germination to flowering: as short as possible

Since he had never grown marijuana before, Leo did his research, consulting grow guides and magazines, as well as numerous online sources, to select the first varieties he tried. By doing a lot of advance research, Leo reduced the trial-and-error elements of growing his first crop as much as possible. You can benefit from Leo's research, too, by trying some of these proven varieties. I've tried, as much as possible, to take the guesswork out of choosing varieties for your first marijuana garden by providing the detail you need to pick the plants that will work best for your climate and growing situation.

I've also tried to simplify the selection process a bit by outlining four basic growing scenarios and proposing varieties that would work well in each scenario. This is just a starting point—only you can determine what really works in your particular scenario, and often this does involve some trial and error. Gardening, as any gardener will tell you, tends to be a crapshoot despite all your experience and study. Like predicting the weather, there are simply too many variables to be 100 percent successful every time. That said, by sharing a first-time grower's successes and setbacks, I hope to give you a head start and reduce as much as possible the trial-and-error parts of your marijuana garden.

Four Basic Growing Scenarios

Based on Leo's experiments, here are four growing scenarios and the varieties that worked best for each one. Of course, you may need to modify your choices based on your particular environment. For example, in climates where there are no frosts, it is possible to grow marijuana continuously all year long. Detailed descriptions of the varieties listed here start on page 66.

- Scenario #1 Inside Only, Year Round, Limited Space: *Lowryder #2 Feminized* and *White Widow*

- Scenario #2 Inside Only, Year Round, Ample Space: *Shiesel* and *White Rhino*

- Scenario #3 Outside, In Season, Limited Space: *BubbleGummer*, *G13*, *Haze Automatic*, *G13 Labs NL Automatic*, *Purple Maroc*, and *Rock Star*

- Scenario #4 Outside, In Season, Ample Space: *Blue Fruit*, *Kalichakra*, *New York City Diesel*, *Satori*, *Sugar Black Rose*, *Super Cali Haze*, and *Super Lemon Haze*

THC AND CBD PERCENTAGES AND THEIR EFFECTS

As mentioned earlier, THC, or tetrahydrocannabinol, is the active ingredient in marijuana that produces the "high." *CBD*, or cannabidiol, is generally regarded as the pain-reducing chemical of the plant. THC and CBD percentages are often cited online in marijuana-growing forums and seed catalogs and are very confusing because the methodology for determining them is not revealed. In other words, the labs that do the tests typically do not reveal how the testing is done and what that percentage reflects. Theoretically the tincture technique used in chapter 10 could give you a rough estimation of THC levels, but I'm not sure the approximate percentages are of any use for the average patient. Since there is so much disparity and confusion over the stated percentages from the various sources, I have decided to omit them from the descriptions on the following pages. Sometimes, in his observations, Leo refers to the different effects produced by the two main species of *Cannabis*, *sativa* and *indica*. This is subjective and imprecise, as any stoner knows, but in general, *sativa* produces more of a "cerebral" high that is mildly hallucinogenic, while *indica* uses "body rushes" that are like waves of pleasure focused below your head.

The Chosen Ones

The varieties that follow are listed in alphabetical order. In each description, I've included details on the species, genetics, characteristics, height, supplier, yield, flowering time to harvest, and Leo's observations. Before I get to the actual varieties, here's some more information about what you'll be reading.

SPECIES: These are all pure *sativa* or *indica*, or various hybrids of *sativa*, *indica*, and *ruderalis*.

GENETICS: Generally, these are the varieties used to produce the listed variety (if known).

CHARACTERISTICS: Any distinctive or noteworthy traits of the variety.

HEIGHT: The mature height of the plants can vary greatly due to different methods of cultivation, so I've used general descriptors: short (two to three feet); medium (three to six feet); and tall (six feet and more).

SUPPLIER: The variety developer or seed bank that sells the seed. All can be contacted though their website.

YIELD: This is approximate and depends on the growing conditions and how large the plants are allowed to grow. In all of these cases, the weight is based on dried, cleaned, and manicured flower tops and not the trim or shade leaves.

FLOWERING OR GROWING TIME TO HARVEST: This is approximate by necessity, since indoor growers can trigger flowering by adjusting the light cycle (see chapter 7). As with any plant, the total outdoor growing time can vary depending on the latitude as well as growing methods and conditions, so there are too many variables to be specific with the total growing time.

LEO'S OBSERVATIONS: Note that Leo did not personally grow all the varieties that follow. But after discussions with other growers, these are the varieties he recommends out of the thousands to choose from.

Once you've chosen the varieties you want to grow, it'll be time to plant your first seeds.

BLUE FRUIT

SPECIES: *Indica* (80%) and *sativa* (20%)

GENETICS: A cross between a purple Mexican variety, a Thai *sativa*, an original Afghani high-yield variety, and 'Blueberry'

CHARACTERISTICS: Sweet and fruity flavor

HEIGHT: Tall outdoors; medium indoors

SUPPLIER: Dinafem Seeds via Attitude Seed Bank

YIELD: Up to 12 ounces per plant

FLOWERING TIME TO HARVEST: 8 to 10 weeks after flowering begins

LEO'S OBSERVATIONS: First developed in Oregon. Sometimes shows deformed leaves. Height needs to be controlled for indoor growing. Humidity should be kept at 50% indoors. Abundant resin production and pleasing mental and physical effects. Fruity flavor with lingering aftertaste.

BLUE RYDER

SPECIES: *Indica*, *sativa*, and *ruderalis*

GENETICS: A cross between 'Lowryder #2' and 'Blueberry'

CHARACTERISTICS: Very potent; autoflowering

HEIGHT: Short

SUPPLIER: See sidebar, page 67

YIELD: About 1 ounce

GROWING TIME TO HARVEST: About 9 weeks from seed

LEO'S OBSERVATIONS: Variable results but excellent medicine.

LEO'S FIRST ATTEMPT AT BREEDING

Near the end of Leo's first growing season, he tried an F1 cross—a first-generation cross between two varieties—between a 'Lowryder #2' male and a 'Blueberry' female. He called this experimental cross 'Blue Ryder'. Upon harvesting, he found that more than half the seeds were too immature to grow but some were the correct mottled brown color of mature seeds. Next time he tries a seed crop, he'll let the seed bracts open and begin to drop their seeds before drying the plant. He learned that you should ignore the usual signs for harvesting flowering tops when growing a seed crop.

Leo and some friends have grown several plants from his 'Blue Ryder' seeds. The results? As Leo put it, "Rather mixed as might be expected. Some plants autoflowered, some didn't, and a few developed freaky, crinkled leaves. The average height was about three feet with many flowering sites." A common and most important feature: They all developed highly potent resinous, flowering tops. One friend told him that 'Blue Ryder' was his favorite medicine. His next step will be to "back-breed" his finest 'Blue Ryder' female to a 'Lowryder #2' male in hopes of stabilizing the autoflower characteristics without losing the rich aroma and potency of this hybrid.

The swollen bracts and brown pistils indicate a top that has set seeds.

BUBBLEGUMMER

SPECIES: *Indica* and *sativa*

GENETICS: Developed from 'BubbleGum'

CHARACTERISTICS: Feminized; distinct bubble-gum flavor

HEIGHT: Medium

SUPPLIER: Female seeds via Attitude Seed Bank

YIELD: About 1 ounce

FLOWERING TIME TO HARVEST: 8 weeks after flowering begins

LEO'S OBSERVATIONS: First developed in Indiana, then further refined in New England and Holland. Seeds grow vigorously. Usually grown indoors. Produces compact resinous flowers.

G13 LABS NL AUTOMATIC

SPECIES: Mostly *indica*; some *sativa* and *ruderalis*

GENETICS: A 'Northern Lights' hybrid with *ruderalis*

CHARACTERISTICS: Feminized; mostly white trichomes

HEIGHT: Short to medium

SUPPLIER: Various via Attitude Seed Bank

YIELD: 3 ounces indoors per plant, much more outdoors

FLOWERING TIME TO HARVEST: 6 to 8 weeks after flowering begins

LEO'S OBSERVATIONS: The yields mentioned by the various suppliers are absurdly high. Also sold as simply *G13*.

HAZE AUTOMATIC

SPECIES: *Ruderalis*, *sativa*, and *indica*

GENETICS: Developed from 'Super Silver Haze'

CHARACTERISTICS: Lemony flavor; compact form; flowering not triggered by the day-night cycle

HEIGHT: Usually under 4 feet

SUPPLIER: Dinafem Seeds via Attitude Seed Bank

YIELD: About 1 to 2 ounces per plant

FLOWERING TIME TO HARVEST: 10 to 11 weeks after flowering begins

LEO'S OBSERVATIONS: Lacks the fruity flavor that many prefer.

KALICHAKRA

SPECIES: *Sativa* and *indica*

GENETICS: A cross between 'Crystal Queen' and 'White Satin'

CHARACTERISTICS: Fruity and floral; resinous and high yielding

HEIGHT: Tall

SUPPLIER: Mandala Seeds via Attitude Seed Bank

YIELD: Up to 16 ounces per plant

FLOWERING TIME TO HARVEST: 10 to 11 weeks after flowering begins

LEO'S OBSERVATIONS: Mold-resistant. Excellent for hot and temperate climates with high humidity.

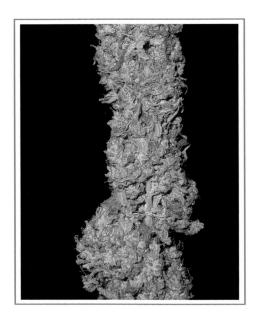

LOWRYDER #2 FEMINIZED

SPECIES: Mostly *indica* with some *ruderalis* for small size

GENETICS: A cross between 'Santa Maria' and 'Lowryder'

CHARACTERISTICS: Autoflowering (not dependent on day/night cycle but flowers automatically when feminized); bushy, very early and prolific flowering

HEIGHT: Short

SUPPLIER: Joint Doctors via Attitude Seed Bank

YIELD: ¼ ounce per plant; much more if grown outdoors in direct light

GROWING TIME TO HARVEST: 9 weeks from seed

LEO'S OBSERVATIONS: Only grown from seeds due to short life cycle. No cloning. Eighteen hours of light daily is best.

NEW YORK CITY DIESEL

SPECIES: *Sativa* (60%) and *indica* (40%)

GENETICS: A cross between 'Sour Diesel' and Afghani and Hawaiian varieties

CHARACTERISTICS: Feminized; needs constant pruning indoors and outdoors; very good producer

HEIGHT: Tall outdoors; medium indoors

SUPPLIER: Soma Seeds

YIELD: Up to 3.5 ounces per plant indoors

FLOWERING TIME TO HARVEST: 10 weeks after flowering begins

LEO'S OBSERVATIONS: Also called 'NYC Diesel' at Attitude Seed Bank. Smells like ripe red grapefruit. *High Times* second-place-cup winner, *sativa* category.

PURPLE MAROC

SPECIES: Mostly *sativa* with some *indica*

GENETICS: Bred from a *sativa* variety called 'Moroccan Ketama'

CHARACTERISTICS: Feminized; designed for outdoor growing; a heavy resin producer

HEIGHT: Medium

SUPPLIER: Female seeds via Attitude Seed Bank

YIELD: High; outdoors 12 to 16 ounces per plant

FLOWERING TIME TO HARVEST: 8 weeks after flowering begins

LEO'S OBSERVATIONS: Prefers sandy soils and needs minimum watering. One seed autoflowered. An easy, short *sativa* with good flavor.

ROCK STAR

SPECIES: *Indica* and *sativa*

GENETICS: A cross between 'Rock Bud' and 'Sensi Star'

CHARACTERISTICS: Can also be pruned and grown indoors

HEIGHT: Tall outdoors; medium indoors

SUPPLIER: Bonguru Beans

YIELD: 16 ounces per plant outdoors

FLOWERING TIME TO HARVEST: 7 to 9 weeks after flowering begins

LEO'S OBSERVATIONS: Copious resin production in the flowers. Good for beginners and easy to manicure.

SATORI

SPECIES: *Sativa* and *indica*

GENETICS: A cross between 'Lucid Dreams' and an unnamed *sativa* hybrid

CHARACTERISTICS: Fruity aroma and flavor

HEIGHT: Tall outdoors; medium indoors

SUPPLIER: Mandala Seeds via Attitude Seed Bank

YIELD: Up to 16 ounces per plant outdoors; up to 9 ounces indoors

FLOWERING TIME TO HARVEST: 10 to 11 weeks after flowering begins

LEO'S OBSERVATIONS: Very easy to grow. It has a sweet and fruity aroma, and it's easy to manicure.

SHIESEL

SPECIES: *Indica* (75%) and *sativa* (25%)

GENETICS: A cross between 'Shiva' and 'New York City Diesel'

CHARACTERISTICS: Fruity aroma and flavor; can also be grown outside

HEIGHT: Medium

SUPPLIER: Bonguru Beans

YIELD: Up to 6 ounces per plant outdoors

FLOWERING TIME TO HARVEST: 8 to 10 weeks after flowering begins

LEO'S OBSERVATIONS: This variety is for the more experienced grower because it's difficult to grow indoors.

SUGAR BLACK ROSE

SPECIES: *Indica* (80%) and *sativa* (20%)

GENETICS: Bred from 'Critical' and 'Black Domina' varieties

CHARACTERISTICS: Feminized; unique and complex aroma

HEIGHT: Medium

SUPPLIER: Delicious Seeds via Attitude Seed Bank

YIELD: 15 ounces per plant

GROWING TIME TO HARVEST: 7 to 8 weeks after flowering begins

LEO'S OBSERVATIONS: Excellent medicinal variety with a high THC content. It is an attractive plant with broad leaves, a gentle musk aroma, and a sweet taste.

SUPER CALI HAZE

SPECIES: Mostly *sativa* with some *ruderalis*

GENETICS: A cross between 'Nirvana Sky', *ruderalis*, and a Colombian *sativa*

CHARACTERISTICS: Feminized; autoflowering

HEIGHT: Tall

SUPPLIER: Short Stuff Seeds via Attitude Seed Bank

YIELD: 4 to 9 ounces per plant

GROWING TIME TO HARVEST: 17 weeks from seed

LEO'S OBSERVATIONS: This flowered very early. Only tried one seed, but it was easy to grow and had a pleasant flavor.

SUPER LEMON HAZE

SPECIES: Mostly *sativa* with some *indica*

GENETICS: A cross between 'Lemon Skunk' and 'Super Silver Haze'

CHARACTERISTICS: Intense lemony flavor; Christmas-tree shape when unpruned

HEIGHT: Very tall

SUPPLIER: Green House Seed Co. via Attitude Seed Bank

YIELD: Up to 3.5 ounces per plant indoors; considerably more outdoors

FLOWERING TIME TO HARVEST: 9 to 10 weeks after flowering begins

LEO'S OBSERVATIONS: Fast growth and large size. Very potent and popular. It needs a lot of nutrients, so fertilize generously.

WHITE RHINO

SPECIES: *Indica* (60%) and *sativa* (40%)

GENETICS: A cross between a United States *indica* and 'White Widow'

CHARACTERISTICS: Can be grown outside as well as inside; trichomes are very white; 'White Rhino' is denser and shorter than 'White Widow'

HEIGHT: Medium

SUPPLIER: Various via Attitude Seed Bank

YIELD: Up to 16 ounces per plant outdoors

FLOWERING TIME TO HARVEST: 8 to 9 weeks after flowering begins

LEO'S OBSERVATIONS: Very prolific flowering and less powerful than 'White Widow'. Huge leaves.

WHITE WIDOW

SPECIES: *Indica* and *sativa*

GENETICS: A cross between Indian, Afghani, and Brazilian varieties

CHARACTERISTICS: Feminized seed; flowering by photoperiod; easy to grow

HEIGHT: Short indoors; tall outdoors

SUPPLIER: Green House Seed Co. via Attitude Seed Bank

YIELD: Up to 5 ounces per plant indoors

FLOWERING TIME TO HARVEST: 8 to 9 weeks after flowering begins

LEO'S OBSERVATIONS: Very famous. So-named because of white trichomes. Compact and dense, with plenty of branching. Supposedly one of the most potent varieties available. Strong odor.

CHAPTER 5

The Growing Begins

From Germination to Sprouted Seedling and Beyond

This chapter covers the procedures for germinating seeds and growing the seedlings until they are large enough to transplant into the containers they will spend the rest of their lives in.

Seed Germination: The Sprouting Embryo Emerges

The elements controlling seed germination are moisture, temperature, oxygen, and the food contained within the seed. The seed absorbs the moisture and swells, food is digested within it, and cell division causes the embryo to grow, splitting the seed coat. The result of the sprouting is essentially a baby seedling. Cannabis seed germination time varies greatly by variety, ranging from a day to a week or more. Temperature is critical—germination is delayed or totally inhibited by cold. Immature seeds, those that are a solid white color, will not germinate. Nor will seeds that are cracked or otherwise damaged. You can germinate your seeds either indoors or outdoors, but Leo and I prefer indoors because the little seedlings are at their most vulnerable stage, and they need protection from high winds and insect pests.

Germination Methods

Growers tend to favor one germination method over others, but they all produce the same result if the previously mentioned elements are present. Here are several methods you can use to make those baby seedlings.

Paper Towel Technique: I think it's important to make sure that the seeds are viable before planting, so I recommend the following technique. Wet two paper towels, squeeze out the excess water, and spread the towels two-sheets thick on a counter. Drop the seeds on the towel, fold it over the seeds, place in a resealable bag, and close the bag. Then move the bag to a warm place (the ideal temperature is 78 degrees Fahrenheit), like the top of your refrigerator or close to an incandescent bulb. Check the results after five days and only plant the seeds that have sprouted. Close up the bag and give any unsprouted seeds another week, checking them daily.

Leo thinks this germination technique is old-fashioned, but admits that it does work. If you use my method, take some care when moving the baby seedlings to the growing medium. Some experts advise you to use tweezers rather than your fingers to move the seedlings because your fingers can kill your seedlings. However, I've always used my fingers and never had a single fatality. These plants are tougher than you think, but if you do use your fingers, wear latex gloves or sterilize your fingers with rubbing alcohol first. I don't like tweezers because it's difficult to control the pressure applied to the seedlings when picking them up, and squeezing them too hard can injure or kill them.

Direct Seeding: *Direct seeding* means that the seeds are germinated in the container where they will spend the rest of their short life. Fill a container with a seed-starting mix or sterile potting soil combined with perlite (four parts soil to one part perlite), moisten the soil, and push a single seed into the soil very close to the top. Sprinkle a little more potting soil over it. Keep the container warm and moist until the seedling sprouts. You can place the container on a heating pad or heating coils to ensure that it's warm, but take care that the heat doesn't dry out the soil. Of course, if the seed doesn't sprout, you have to start all over again, which is why I prefer to sprout the seeds before actually placing them in soil.

Rockwool Single Block: The rockwool single-block system for germination is a large tray with rockwool cubes with a prepunched hole in the top of each one. (*Rockwool* is a combination of melted rock and sand that is spun to make fibers that are formed into different shapes and sizes.) These work fine, but are overkill for the twelve-plant grower, as the trays hold a hundred or more cubes.

Peat or Plastic Pots: Two additional systems are better for the home gardener. Peat pots filled with seed-starting mix or potting soil mixed with perlite work well except they tend to dry out too quickly. The small, two-inch plastic pots in which commercial nurseries sell small bedding plants also work well and don't dry out like the peat pots do.

Leo's Germination Technique: Leo dislikes the rockwool single-block system because, of course, it's not organic. He suggests this alternate method:

1. Lightly scar the seeds on a fine sandpaper nail file by rolling the seed over it with your index finger. "Lightly" is the operative word here—you don't want to injure the seed.

2. Soak the seeds overnight in a small glass of water (about a cup); do not soak for more than twenty-four hours.

3. Insert the seeds into root plugs (also called grow plugs—they are a spongelike material made from composted tree bark and organic materials). Leo prefers Rapid Rooter, made by General Hydroponics.

4. Wait two to ten days for sprouting to occur.

5. Transfer the plugs to peat pots and place under compact fluorescent lights on a cycle of eighteen hours on and six hours off.

6. Water daily with tap water.

As you can see, there are numerous methods. Call me old-fashioned, but I recommend my paper-towel process because you can easily separate the fertile seeds from the infertile ones.

A seedling emerges from the seed in a peat pot, which it will live in until being transplanted into a plastic pot.

The Care and Feeding of Your Little Sprouts

Shortly after emerging, your seedlings are at their most vulnerable stage and are susceptible to a wide range of dangers. By far, the biggest problem I've had with seedlings of any species is damping-off. The warm, wet conditions necessary for germination and initial growth are the perfect environment for fungi (especially *Pythium*) that attack the seedlings and cause them to topple over. If the seedlings do that, they are lost and you have to start again. To protect seedlings from damping-off, be sure to have lots of air circulation around the seedlings. Remember, if you do everything else right but forget to provide plenty of air movement, you will still get damping-off. Besides, the moving air will strengthen the stems, which is beneficial. Also be careful not

A three-week-old plant outdoors in the early morning sun.

to overwater seedlings—for example, don't let the seedlings' pots sit in a saucer full of water. Make sure that the growing medium drains quickly, or the water will drown the roots because the roots won't receive the oxygen they need. Too much water contributes to the damping-off problem and can also promote diseases that cause root rot.

Other difficulties you might encounter with new seedlings include cats grazing on them or the possibility that the seedlings might burn under the lights. You want the seedlings as close to the light source as possible so they won't get "leggy" and fall over, so put the palm of your hand where you want the top of the seedlings to be. If you can keep it there for a minute without burning your hand, the seedlings won't burn, either.

Many growers squabble over whether to fertilize the seedlings at this tender moment in their lives. There are special seedling fertilizers, but you must be careful to use fertilizer of any kind sparingly because it can burn or kill your expensive crop. Dilute, dilute, dilute—if you are using any type of fertilizer on very young plants. You can always use more, but it's impossible to remove what you've already overfed them. Leo's take on this debate is "don't fertilize until the seedlings are at least two weeks old," and I agree with him.

Give seedlings at least sixteen hours of light daily until they are large and sturdy enough to be transplanted. This is another topic of much debate: how long to keep young seedlings in the initial growing medium before transplanting them. Well, you want the roots developed enough that they combine with the soil into a small root ball, but not so cramped in the pot that the roots are bound up and have to be cut apart. Yes, the varieties develop differently and all the environmental factors come into play: the type and size of the initial container, the light spectrum and intensity, the plant's vigor, and nutrients. But generally speaking, when you have four sets of fully developed leaves (excluding the "false" or "seed" leaves—the round cotyledon leaves), you should make your plan for the total body transplant.

Transplanting Your Seedlings: Freedom to the Roots

Oh, the sheltered lives your plants are leading. They're like spoiled kids who get everything they want and never have to do chores. Fortunately, you don't have to buy them video games and iPods. But they're growing fast now, generating roots quickly, and you don't want to take a chance on inhibiting their vegetative growth by restricting their root growth. So it's transplant time, and here's how to do it right.

Use the same type of potting soil in the new pots that you used for the seedlings, except if you've used seed-starting mix. In that case, switch to potting soil and perlite in a four-to-one ratio. And be sure to keep both the seedlings

Transplanting is quite easy and not traumatic to the plants.

and the soil uniformly moist in the new pot. If you are removing plants from little plastic pots, squeeze the pots and tap them on the bottom to loosen the root ball. The seedling and root ball should slip right out. Disturb the root ball as little as possible and don't let the root ball dry out.

Some growers like to trim or prune the roots before transplanting, but why? You're not creating a bonsai marijuana plant, and the plant needs those roots. I have yet to figure out the logic behind this, since you will always be transplanting to a larger container. Many growers exaggerate the difficulty of transplanting and overemphasize the need to reduce the light afterward to give the plant time to recover from the supposed trauma of the process. This is nonsense. If you are careful, the plant will not suffer from any shock or trauma. There also is no need to reduce the intensity of light to give the plant time to recover. What is the plant recovering from, anyway? It's not like you're brutally ripping it out of the soil and roughly pushing it into a larger pot and then stomping on it. This is marijuana, the original renegade, not an orchid. I remember taking dozens of seedlings in small pots, moving them more than a hundred miles in a dark van, and then transplanting them directly into prepared garden soil. They all survived and flourished because they had been hardened off. Transplanting is not traumatic unless you're moving plants from indoor situations to outdoor ones without proper preparation.

Hardening Off

If you plan to continue growing under lights, move the transplants under your lighting system designed for vegetative growth, paying particular attention to their distance from the bulbs to avoid burning them. But if you plan to move any of the transplants outside, there is another necessary step in the procedure: *hardening-off*. This means preparing the plants for a totally new environment that is far different from the sheltered one they've enjoyed since birth. It's a jungle out there, and you've got to get them ready for it. If you're going to be using a covered raised bed, your plants won't need much hardening off at all, if any. But moving them directly

into full sun and wind can be traumatic without proper preparation.

Consider the difference between indoor lighting and full sunlight. Sunlight is measured by *lux*, which equals lumens per square meter. HID lamps give figures in lumens, which is just the power of the initially transmitted light, not the illumination as perceived by the human eye. When moved the necessary distance away from the plants, the lux drops radically from the initial lumens emitted by the bulb. Taking into consideration that the lux of sunlight varies all over the world depending on latitude and weather, sunlight is, roughly speaking, about ten times the intensity of HID-emitted light. You shouldn't place plants conditioned to indoor lighting directly into full sunlight—they will be fried, especially by the sun's intense ultraviolet light. The wind is also a factor in moving the transplants outdoors. Sure, your plants have experienced breezes in your grow room, possibly as strong as five miles per hour. How well do you think they're going to do in the sixty miles per hour winds of a fierce thunderstorm, or even winds one-third that strong? They're going to be whipped to death unless you adapt them first.

Start the hardening-off process by moving the plants into full shade for a day or two, then into partial shade for a few more days, and finally into full sun for a few hours each day. Gradually lengthen the amount of time they are in full sun each day. You are slowly adapting the plants to full sunlight, and the breezes are toughening the stems. Of course, if really high winds develop, place the plants behind a windbreak, or bring them back inside if it gets really bad in their new environment. The length of the hardening-off process is usually a week to ten days. Experience will teach you how this process works, and it's better to err on the side of lengthy hardening-off than to risk burning your plants.

Now that you've coddled your plants along, spending money on them and wining and dining them, it's time to shift the responsibility to their strong branches and prepare for the payback. There's a lot of work ahead for the faithful worker herbs as they enter the exciting horticultural phase known as—drum roll—vegetative growth.

CHAPTER 6

A "Noted Weed" Triumphant

The Growing Season

Shakespeare once wrote that marijuana is a "noted weed" and, as mentioned in chapter 1, it is also a renegade—one of the few plants to return to nature after being cultivated. The marijuana plants concealed in Leo's backyard are not really weeds, but rather valuable commercial crops with beneficial properties. Despite their renegade status, there are a number of needs that your plants have following the initial transplanting, including air circulation, fertilizer, pruning, and a careful daily inspection for pests and problems. If you want your plants to flourish through the growing season to the cultivation stage, you'll need to understand these needs well.

Air Circulation

This is not going to be much of a problem outdoors because marijuana is very tolerant of fluctuations in temperature and humidity when it is not enclosed; breezes and natural convection (heated air rising) will move the air around, even if the plants are concealed within an urban garden. But growing indoors is a different story because of the artificial environment you have built in a rather small space.

It is essential to have an adequate supply of fresh air (an intake) and a ventilation system that includes an exhaust fan to keep the air circulating at all times. Your goals with your air circulation system are

- to stabilize humidity;

- to prevent mold from growing; and

- to replenish oxygen and nitrogen, which are used by the plants to grow.

Because hot air rises, the intake should be at ground level and the exhaust fan should be at ceiling level. In between you will need one or more fans constantly moving the air around. For the indoor grow room, there are three types of fans to consider:

Stand fans: This is exactly what the name implies—a fan on top of a pole or stand, usually with a sixteen-inch diameter. The advantage to these is their height, which can blow air over the top of the plants. The disadvantage is their cost—they can be expensive.

Oscillating fans: These fans, mounted in vertical tubes called "blower towers" about forty inches high, can rotate at least 180 degrees, providing a broad sweep of air movement. Here too, the drawback is their expense.

Box fans: These range in diameter from ten to twenty inches and provide ample air circulation at the most reasonable price. In all of my growing rooms, I used two twenty-inch box fans and always had good air circulation.

Cooling the Grow Room

If you are growing indoors during the summer, the lights you use may produce so much heat that even ventilation will not be enough to control it. The optimum temperature for your grow room is 75 degrees Fahrenheit, so getting close to that is your goal. If your house uses refrigerated air conditioning, placing an exhaust fan to suck cool air from your house into the grow room may be a possible solution to overheating, especially if there are no air conditioning vents in the room. Small, single-room air conditioners can also be installed in windows or walls, and can be set to counter the heat buildup from the lights and fan motors. They also will provide air circulation. Adjusting the lighting cycle to growing only at night when the house is cooler should also be considered.

If your house uses evaporative coolers, just remember that they will add some humidity to your growing environment, which will be combined with the humidity caused by plant transpiration. Adequate ventilation should control this additional humidity, especially in small grow rooms. Some growers in dry climates install portable swamp coolers—smaller, self-contained versions of the evaporative coolers used on the roof of the house.

Humidity Control

The optimum amount of humidity in a grow room is 60 percent, but marijuana can thrive in much drier conditions than that. But in moist environments, such as western Oregon, humidity buildup can be the source of mold in the grow room and can cause a condition known as powdery mildew (more on this in chapter 9). To prevent such conditions from ruining your plants, you may need to install a dehumidifier in your grow room. They range from a mini-dehumidifier suitable for a closet or small grow room to more expensive units for large rooms that can cost several hundred dollars. Dehumidifiers are rated according to the volume of water they can collect from the air into their tanks (which must be emptied when full). So the mini-dehumidifiers collect about four pints of water, while the larger ones have a capacity of sixty to seventy pints. Obviously the smaller the collection tank, the more often it must be emptied.

Watering

Novice growers are often so worried about their plants drying out that they keep them constantly saturated with water, which prevents the roots from getting the oxygen they need. Indoors or out, there is a simple solution to this problem—placing the growing pots in saucers or shallow waterproof plastic containers to catch the water that drains from the pot. If water is standing in the saucers, the plant does not need watering. If it is dry,

water carefully—the water that accumulates in the saucer should never be more than one-half inch deep. At this level, only a very small amount of water will wick up to the plants.

Outdoor plants transpire so fast during the summer that they must be watered at least daily, depending upon the size of the container they are in, how large the plants are, and the temperature and relative humidity. Obviously, if it rains a lot where you live, you will not need to water as much. This takes constant vigilance and Leo complained to me more than once that he felt chained to his growing operation. "I can't even take a few days' vacation," he said, "because I can't trust anyone to take care of the plants if I leave." Leo doesn't mean that he worries about a security breach if he leaves, but rather that he doesn't know anyone with enough experience growing container plants to tend his garden, except me, and if I took on that project, I would have to camp at Leo's house. I told him that I feel the same way about my traditional garden, which has food plants in the ground but some herbs, chiles, and ornamental plants in containers ranging from one gallon to thirty or more gallons. I, too, feel uncomfortable about leaving my house for any extended period of time because all potential house sitters must have experience with both pets and plants, and house sitters like that are hard to find. So, my wife and I must stay home during the summer just like Leo. The thought of not having a garden has never been seriously considered in my family.

One possible solution to the need for constantly watering the potted plants is, of course, growing the plants in rows in a vegetable garden or in elevated beds watered by soaker hoses. Watering those plants is easier because it is done less frequently and takes much less time. That said, more care must be taken in concealing them, so this is not an option for many home growers.

Fertilizing the Growing Plants

Marijuana thrives on nitrogen during vegetative growth, and home growers must apply it regularly to the plants over the growing season. However, take care not to overfertilize—it's one of the most common mistakes home growers make, and it's easy to burn the plants from the application of heavily concentrated nitrogen. If the leaf tips begin to curl or turn brown, or if there are brown blotches on the leaves, that's a signal that you're giving them too much nitrogen and the result is a condition called—appropriately enough—*fertilizer burn*. My typical response when this happens is to flush the container with water several times and stop fertilizing for the season unless the recovered plant begins to show symptoms of underfertilization: leaves that lose their bright green color and turn pale.

Maintaining pH

The pH, or the relative acidity or alkalinity of your growing medium, should remain as close to neutral as possible, which is seven on a scale of zero to fourteen, where zero is the most acidic. You can measure it easily with test strips (which are not precisely accurate) or with a waterproof pH pen, which is more expensive but easier to use. Gardening shops carry products to adjust the pH of the medium your plants are growing in, but be sure to follow the instructions carefully, or you'll be stuck in the loop of increasing acidity one day and alkalinity the next. An acidic growing medium locks up nutrients in acid salts, resulting in curling leaves, reduced flowering, and a greatly diminished yield. Too much alkalinity causes chlorosis, the yellowing of the leaves, which interferes with photosynthesis, thus reducing plant vigor and growth.

Sensible Insect Control

Both Leo and I watch for insects and diseases, but marijuana is hardy and he hasn't found any sign of disease or the most common plant pests—whiteflies, aphids, mealybugs, and spider mites. The only pest that Leo has found on his outdoor plants was a single grasshopper a quarter inch long. He freed it into the nonmarijuana section of his garden. Small grasshoppers and crickets can be controlled by sprinkling the pots and leaves lightly with diatomaceous earth, a mostly harmless, abrasive powder that is sold in gardening shops and herb stores. Wear a dust mask when applying it, and don't use it in areas your pets frequent. It is a mechanical insecticide, which means it doesn't poison the insects but rather absorbs lipids (fatty acids) from the insects' exoskeletons, causing them to dehydrate. Diatomaceous earth is a good example of a natural (not humanmade) insecticide.

Leo fervently believes in organic gardening and mostly I agree with him, except when it comes to controlling insect infestations. A word of warning here: the terms "natural" and "organic" are often bandied about in gardening discussions, and many gardeners assume that if things come from nature rather than being manufactured, they are obviously better. Here are some "natural" things to avoid: nicotine sulfate, an organic pesticide, is the most hazardous botanical insecticide available to home gardeners. Never use it. Rotenone, a natural insecticide permitted in organic gardening, is highly toxic to fish and is classified by the World Health Organization as moderately hazardous. Don't even think about it. Even pyrethrum, widely considered to be the safest organic insecticide, from seemingly innocent daisies, can easily kill bees. So, would I recommend Raid Flying Insect Spray over any of those to eliminate whitefly? Definitely, if applied carefully with a very light push on the button.

Leo (with my hands assisting) must constantly prune his *sativa* plants to control growth.

Pruning: *Cannabis* Contortionists

Pruning is simply trimming a growing plant to modify its form, which is also known as the plant's *habit*. With marijuana, pruning can begin when the plant is a seedling with only four or five sets of leaves. Growers, using their thumb and forefinger, pinch off the top growing bud, causing branches to form earlier than normal and making the plant shorter and bushier. This is called *pinching back*, because you use your thumb and forefinger to pinch off an emerging stem when the plant is young. Your grandmother can show you how to do it with her begonias. Some purists state that pinching back with your fingers "helps

seal the wound" and thus is less damaging to the plants than using a razor blade or scissors. Well, you can always pinch the scissor-cut stem with your finger! You shouldn't be pruning a mature, woody stem anyway but rather new growth. This is important when growing under lights because of the inverse square law mentioned earlier—you have to keep the plants as close to the lights as possible without burning them in order to achieve maximum vegetative growth, even if it's more lateral than vertical. The more vegetation you have, the more flowers you will also have.

Constant pruning of the *sativa* varieties and crosses was Leo's biggest challenge, and for outdoor growing it will be yours, too. Unlike a hedge of roses, which can be effectively pruned by simply running an electric or gas-powered pruning saw over the tops of all the plants (heresy, but it works), you must carefully cut flowerless (as yet) growth from the top of marijuana plants. Leo's difficulty was caused by waiting too long to prune because he didn't think the plants would get so tall.

You should never remove more than 25 percent of the total plant when pruning, and you should remember that you prune just-emerged stems and not single leaves. The plant needs the large leaves for good photosynthesis and vigorous growth. And once blooming has started, stop pruning all together. But all of these comments would be mitigated by your selection of smaller, *indica*-oriented varieties. Then you wouldn't have much, if any, pruning to do. *Topping*, or pruning the central growing stem, however, is a technique to consider with

some *sativa* varieties because it can cause the development of more growing tips on lateral branches that turn into flower tops, thus increasing the yield from a single plant. Leo's take on topping, however, is that it's not necessarily effective. You might get more tops but the same yield, he told me, thus illustrating the ongoing debates about plant care that occur from grower to grower. I'm pretty sure that no scientific experiments have ever been conducted, but this subject is covered in detail in the next chapter.

There are many different ways of pruning marijuana plants, even to the point of pruning to specifically fit them on a trellis, for example. You won't have too much use for such trellising techniques, but you might think about *training*, or bending the plants, with the help of twine. To train a plant, you bend a branch that's almost vertical into a horizontal position to allow more sunlight to reach the smaller flowers. These plants are being *espaliered*, or trained to grow on a flat plane, like against a wall. Some growers have turned their plants into corkscrews or circles, but the most common technique gives the plants the shape of the letter "S" to reduce their height; just bend strong wire to whatever shape you want and tie the marijuana plants into that shape.

My compost container may be humble, but it works. I used steel-mesh wire screening for the frame, thick black plastic sheeting on the inside, and a paving stone to weigh the plastic down.

Composting for the Marijuana Bed

Home gardeners blessed with adequate security may want to grow directly in garden soil. And growing in garden soil—for, say, planting marijuana amid corn or tomatoes—means that organic matter must be added to the soil in some manner for aeration and good drainage. I believe that one of the major factors in creating a great marijuana garden is the addition of compost to the garden soil, which improves workability, water-holding capability, drainage, and the fertility of the soil. When I was growing in the barn/greenhouse, I did not have adequate amounts of compost to treat the soil, so I depended upon aged steer manure, which worked well. But the home grower of twelve or more plants will have an excellent opportunity to use compost because of the small number of plants. Many gardeners have no choice about composting because many landfills across the country do not accept organic yard refuse such as grass clippings. Thus, composting is a necessity.

Composting is simply the process of organic material decomposing into humus, with the help of microorganisms, insects, earthworms, and water. Also necessary is oxygen, for anaerobic (without oxygen) decomposition is a slow process that causes foul odors. A compost pile is simple to maintain and an important factor in the success of the in-ground marijuana garden. (If you are *only* growing marijuana, you can buy bagged, composted, and sterilized steer manure from a nursery or gardening supply store and skip the compost pile.)

How to Compost

A few criteria are essential for a good compost pile: ample available water, an inconspicuous location convenient to the garden, and at least six hours of sunlight a day or a high daily average summer temperature. A compost pile can be just that—a pile of organic material. However, the pile can be a bit sloppy and difficult to control, so most gardeners prefer to use containers or bins for composting.

Choose a container: Containers can be constructed from a wide variety of materials, including wire screening, wood, cinder blocks or bricks without mortar, and snow fencing. In all cases, the compost container should be enclosed on three sides, leaving the front and top open. The ideal pile in a bin or container is 3 feet high by 3 feet wide. Anything larger is difficult to turn and tends to compact too much, preventing oxygen from reaching all parts of the pile. If you have too much organic material, start another pile.

Add dissimilar materials in layers: For example, the pile should not consist solely of green grass clippings, which tend to pack together and prevent air circulation. Rather, the clippings should be interspersed with layers of other materials. Shredding materials into tiny particles with a mechanical shredder is overrated. Yes, shredding makes the pile smaller, but it is not necessary for large, soft materials such as weed stems or rotting heads of cabbage. Many sources state that the compost pile needs manure from herbivores in order to add sufficient nitrogen and make the pile heat up. Actually, green matter such as garden trimmings will do a good job when applied in a ratio of one part green (nitrogen-rich) material to three parts brown (dried, carbon-rich) material (including dry grass clippings).

Sift the pile: Some gardeners sift the compost from the bins through a one-half-inch mesh screen and return larger particles to the pile for further decomposition. This was my father in action as Garden Commander. I can't tell you how many hundreds of cubic yards of compost my brother and I screened during the many summers of our gardening indentured servitude.

Maintain the pile: The pile should be watered often (depending on your climate), and turned over with a garden fork at least twice during the season. If you live in a moist climate, you probably don't need to cover it because the pile will retain enough moisture on its own. But if you live in a dry climate, cover the pile with a sheet of black plastic and weigh down the cover with bricks or rocks to contain the moisture.

THE GOOD AND THE BAD COMPOSTING CANDIDATES

These green materials make good compost: fresh marijuana trimmings that you don't want to ingest but you don't want to throw away either, corn stalks and leaves, garden plants killed by frost, kitchen scraps (fruits and vegetables), and freshly trimmed tree leaves.

These brown materials make good compost: eggshells, coffee grounds, aged manure from herbivores, dry grass clippings, pine needles, sawdust, shredded newspaper (but not the color sections), straw, and dried weeds without seeds.

These materials are unacceptable for compost: bones, branches from trees and shrubs, diseased garden plants, fats and grease, grass clippings treated with herbicides, kitty litter, magazine pages, manure from carnivores (and pets), meat, plastics, synthetic products, wood ashes, and dead animals.

Apply the compost: Compost should be applied at the rate of one to four bushels (32.5 to 130 liters) per 100 square feet of garden, assuming that you are planting the marijuana among other plants. If you are only growing marijuana, scale this back to half a bushel (about 16 liters) per 25 square feet. Then rototill the compost into the soil. Lazy gardeners like me will skip the mesh screening and let the rototiller do a soil screening.

Composting Problems and Solutions

Although composting is usually a simple and straightforward process, occasionally some problems will arise. Here's how to deal with them.

Strong odor: The pile is too wet or has insufficient oxygen. Add dry materials and turn the pile.

Damp but no noticeable heat: There is insufficient nitrogen. Add grass clippings or other green matter.

Dry but not composting: It's rotting. Water the pile until water runs out of the bottom and keep it as wet as possible.

Hot and steaming: Turn the pile weekly.

Ammonia odor: There is too much nitrogen. Add sawdust, dry leaves, or other high-carbon materials such as dried grass clippings, and turn the pile.

The Daily Inspection

No matter what your growing scenario—indoors, outdoors, in containers, or in beds—you've got to keep an eye on your plants. Inspect them during your daily watering, or if it has just rained on your plants outside, inspect them after it stops. This is what to watch for (see chapter 9 for a detailed discussion of pests and problems if you notice any of the changes below):

• change in leaf color,

• insects or signs of insect damage,

• wilting plants, and

• wind damage.

If you follow this daily inspection plan, your growing scenario will support vigorous vegetative growth that will lead to a successful harvest. But before you break out the harvesting clippers, let's move on to the all-important step of marijuana flowering.

CHAPTER 7

Les Bonnes Fleurs de Marijuana

Or, the Good Flowers of Marijuana

The vegetative growth of marijuana seems to take forever, but be patient, for the most exciting part of growing the crop is on its way. Even seasoned growers get a thrill when the first flowers appear on the plants—male flowers included! In this chapter, I will cover preflowering indications, how to determine the gender of your plants ("sexing them," in the vernacular), outdoor versus indoor flowering, female flowers and creating *sinsemilla*, flowering nutrients, maximizing flower production, male flowering and producing seeds, making clones as a substitute for seeds, and whether or not to flush the plant containers before the harvest.

Preflowering Indications

During the four to eight months of vegetative growth, your plants will add more leaves and stems and grow very quickly. You will see new leaf growth starting at the nodes between the main stem and the first branches. In marijuana cultivation, this is called *calyx development*, which will soon become lateral or secondary branching, meaning not only more branches and leaves, but also flowers. (The *calyx* is defined as

the bud, which will eventually form into flowers.) Calyx development and lateral branching are the first indications that your plants are approaching maturity, and a sign that flowering will happen soon. Now you should pay close attention to the soon-to-be-apparent gender of your plants.

Sexing Your Plants

Your goal is to produce unpollinated female plants, or *sinsemilla*, meaning flowers without seeds. To accomplish this, you have to remove and destroy all the male plants before they flower and spread their pollen. Here's how to distinguish the males from the females early so that you are not surprised by pollen all over your female plants.

Height: If you are growing several plants of the same variety, the taller plants will generally be the males, so you should separate them from the others and watch them carefully. (They are taller so they can spread pollen more efficiently to the females below them.)

Calyx examination: Males tend to form flowers before the females do, so using a magnifying glass, examine the calyxes of all the plants starting lateral branching. If the calyx is raised on a short stem, it is probably male and if there is no stem, it is probably female.

Force-flowering: This may be one of the most reliable of the early sexing methods. Take cuttings of the ends of calyxes that have turned into lateral branching, place them in jars of water, label them and the mother plants you took the cuttings from, and set them apart from the other plants under lights with a cycle of twelve hours of light and twelve hours of darkness. This will trigger or force the flowering of the cuttings before the main plants flower and will give you a head start determining which gender you have.

These three methods are not 100 percent accurate, but they will give you some advance indication. If you continue to observe the lateral branches, you can positively identify the emerging male and female flowers.

Here the first female flowers emerge.

Considered by growers to be useless and usually destroyed when identified, male plants and their flowers contribute half of the genes that control important developments like resin production, so don't be too quick about killing them.

Males look like pods, females look like antennae. The male flowers have rounded sacs, contain pollen, and hang down, while the females have erect, usually white hairs called *pistils* that are sticky, receive the pollen, and look like a butterfly's antennae.

Male flowers usually develop first and more quickly than females. Compare the flowers on your plants to the photos at left and you will soon recognize the differences between the flowers and be able to sex your plants early and easily.

Except for producing pollen to create seeds for future growing (see page 103) male plants are of no use to you. They have virtually no THC in their flowers or leaves, so either move the plants to the compost pile or put them in a trash bag and dispose of them.

Outdoor versus Indoor Flowering

If your plants are grown outdoors, you have no control over the flowering cycle, which is triggered by the days becoming shorter and the nights longer—the seasonal change from summer to fall. This is called the *photoperiod* and is measured by the day/night hours. A photoperiod of 14/10 (that is, fourteen day hours, ten night hours) means vegetative growth, while the flowering photoperiod begins at 12/12. Outdoors, depending upon the latitude where you live, 12/12 occurs between September and November. For an annual plant like marijuana, vegetative growth outdoors needs the most light possible, so they reach that peak during the long summer days. But after the summer solstice, the days begin shortening as the equinox approaches. As soon as the equinox occurs, the trigger is pulled on the female plants and flowering begins.

Imagine being able to do that continuously all year long. You can—indoors. This is why Leo has an outdoor/indoor operation. Outdoors, he has about a five-month growing window; indoors, it's twelve, if he wants it to be. Indoors, by adjusting the timer on your lights, you can control the flowering and even trigger it once you see calyx development and lateral branching.

The key to flowering on a 12/12 cycle in your grow room is that you must have total darkness during the twelve hours the lights are off. This is why your grow room must be lightproof so that no light comes in through cracks, under the door, or through inadequately shaded windows. Even a small desk light at the other side of the room can disrupt the 12/12 cycle, and so can light that shines into the room if you open the door to check on your plants. Just leave them alone during the twelve hours of darkness and they will flower perfectly.

Flowering Female Plants and Creating *Sinsemilla*

Once you have removed the male plants and your females start flowering, the intense flowering will seem unstoppable. Furiously seeking pollen, the male-deprived females mostly stop vegetative growth except for a few small leaves that form on the *colas* (Spanish for "tails"), or spiked flower clusters (called "buds" by the botanically challenged).

In his grow room, Leo has installed high-pressure sodium lights, and their orange-tinted glow resembles the autumn sun, with yellow, orange, and red predominating. With a 12/12 cycle and the autumn light, floral hormones are triggered, and the flowering begins in earnest. You could also add a halide light to the room to increase total light intensity, but most growers don't think that's necessary in Leo's setup because his sodium lights are 600 watts. If they were only 250 watts, a halide

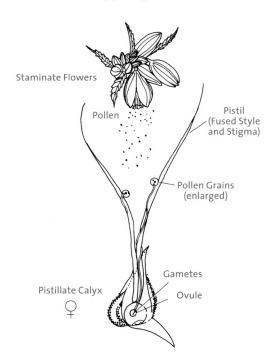

Staminate Flowers

Pollen

Pistil
(Fused Style
and Stigma)

Pollen Grains
(enlarged)

Gametes

Ovule

Pistillate Calyx
♀

The staminate, or male, flower (top) releases pollen to pollinate the pistillate, or female, flower (bottom).

Pistillate Flower

Staminate Flower

Hermaphroditic flowers. The female plant has grown male flowers in an attempt at self-pollination.

Your eyes will see this differently, but the camera captures the strange bronze color of the flowers and leaves under the high-pressure sodium lights.

light would help increase the number of flowers. (When I was growing under grow-light fluorescents during the Paleolithic era, I put my plants on a 16/8 day-night cycle for the vegetative growth stage and then switched to a 12/12 cycle to induce flowering. That worked well, especially considering the inferior light I provided for them.) Marijuana has incredible adaptability and it purely loves to breed. That said, my yields were miniscule compared to Leo's, so my point is this: Use the highest wattage of lights for flowering that you can. Just make sure that they don't overheat your grow room.

After you have removed all the male plants and the females are flowering profusely, you are now growing *sinsemilla*, and for the home grower it means that flowering will continue almost indefinitely because the plant is not setting fruit—the seeds, in this case. If seeds were being produced, the plants' energy would be devoted to that and flowering would cease once each plant had reached its maximum weight in seeds. But without seeds, flowering continues until it peaks and you can begin the harvest. This is covered in detail in the next chapter.

Flowering Nutrients

After flowering begins, the marijuana plants need less nitrogen and more phosphorous and potassium, so it's time to switch your fertilizer. If you are using a water-soluble chemical fertilizer, you should change from a nitrogen-heavy NPK formula of 30-20-20 or 20-15-15 to one of 15-30-30. Do not apply the fertilizer at full strength but rather half-strength so you don't give the plants a chemical burn. For example, if the fertilizer instructions call for a dilution factor of one tablespoon of fertilizer per gallon of water, mix the tablespoon in *two* gallons of water.

If you are growing organically, there are specific fertilizers you can use. Leo swears by FoxFarms Tiger Bloom, made by FoxFarm Soil & Fertilizer Company. It is not as strong as the chemical fertilizer mentioned above, so you have to apply more of it more often, but it is a liquid fertilizer that can be used in any growing medium, including garden soil, container growing media, and hydroponic setups. Just follow the instructions on the container.

Maximizing Flower Production

Two suggested methods for increasing THC production or potency in *sinsemilla* include girdling the plant's stem with a knife or cracking it with your hands—the concept being that the plant will react to this attack by making more psychotropic resin to protect itself. One problem: These methods simply don't work.

The key to unlocking maximum resin is not trying to make the THC more powerful, but simply producing more flowering tops before the harvest. And that's why the main methods for maximizing flower production are pruning and topping, limbing, and crimping, bending, and tying-down.

For cutting the plant with any of these methods, have one set of scissors or clippers for outside and another for inside, and don't mix them up. It is standard procedure to sterilize them with a flame or isopropyl alcohol each time you use them, but I never did and never had a problem. Do keep them sharp, however, because they'll cause less damage to plant tissues if they're sharp. Another alternative is to use single-edged razor blades.

Pruning and Topping

I discussed pruning in chapter 6 as a method to keep the size of your plants manageable. But pruning and topping, a form of pruning, are also used to increase the number of flowering tops on your plants.

Unless you grow one of those midget varieties like the *ruderalis* cross 'Lowryder #2', some amount of pruning early on during the plants' growth will probably be necessary. Pruning both controls height and promotes branching. Just ask Leo. When he pruned his *sativas*, he was merely trying to limit his plants to the vertical dimension of his urban garden rather than promote branching, but, of course, pruning does both. It also tends to delay flowering if done extensively or too late in the plants' growth cycle. The basic method of pruning

focuses its energy on the top parts of the plant where the light (natural or artificial) shines the brightest and the flowers have the best chance to be pollinated by pollen blowing in the wind.

Limbing is not a shock to the plants, whereas removing the large, lower "shade" or "fan" leaves too soon is a shock because they provide a large amount of food to the plant via photosynthesis. These leaves, which are the largest on your plants and are on the lower one-third of their height, eventually turn yellow and fall off the plant. Growers in regions with high humidity remove these leaves as soon as the yellow color appears, because they know it indicates that photosynthesis from that leaf has ceased, and they don't want the dying leaf to attract fungal spores or insect pests.

Crimping, Bending, and Tying Down

Crimping, also called *cracking* or *supercropping*, is the technique of using two hands to twist a branch and produce an internal wound so that it will develop multiple branches from the region of the wound. This should only be done during vegetative growth because it would inhibit flowering if done too late. *Bending* is simply pulling branches down so they are parallel to the ground. Growers usually use string to *tie down* the branches to keep them in place. If you crimp the branches in two or three places on a long stem, bending occurs naturally—you won't have to tie down the

used to promote flowering is called *topping* by growers and *meristem pruning* by botanists. By removing—taking the top off (hence, *topping*)—the main growing stem or *meristem*, the plant becomes bushier, growing more branches that are points for increased flower production. But it also can inhibit flowering if done too late in the plant's life, so if you're going to top the plant, do it early in the vegetative growth stage.

Limbing

Limbing is the removal of the lower, often small and atrophied, branches that, because of shading by the upper branches of the plant, are spindly and will not produce floral clusters. Once these lower limbs are removed, the plant

Fan leaves near a flowering top.

branches. The purpose of bending is twofold: to reduce vertical growth and to expose more of the plant's surface to maximum light so more flower tops will be produced. Leo prefers to tie down the limbs because it's less risky than crimping them. Here's why.

After you switch to a 12/12 growing cycle and flowering begins in earnest, you may assume that all vegetative growth halts and just the flowers grow. But this is not the case. There is an overlap, and some vegetative growth continues, so you can expect at least two, if not three, more weeks of vertical growth from the plants. But if you are growing indoors, you may have run out of space for this growth, which is why Leo and many other growers tie down their tops with string or wire so they are horizontal to the ground.

The new flowers at the nodes will grow toward the light, producing many smaller tops. You will not have the one huge top, or *cola*, that you expected, but the total volume and weight of the harvest will be about the same.

As flowering continues with the tops tied down, the larger leaves will, of course, being phototropic, turn toward the light, blocking much of it from reaching the lower flower tops. These are not the lower fan leaves discussed earlier, but the continuing vegetative growth mentioned above that continues with the flowering. Now, some growers suggest that you should remove the larger leaves so that the light will reach the middle of the plant. But remember the inverse square law—those tops are probably getting one-fourth the intensity of the tops nearest the light, and some of that is being blocked. Those fan leaves are the main photosynthesis producers for the plant—the ones that provide the plant the nourishment it needs so the tops can continue to grow and produce resin. They also store the sugars that are essential for continued flower development.

To remove or not to remove, that is the first question. Some experts recommend removing the offending fan leaves and other say leave them on the plant to fuel the upper tops. At least one expert suggests cutting the top fan leaves in half with scissors, providing more light but still helping the flowers form. Leo's theory is that the lower flowers won't develop that much anyway, so stop worrying about them. He thinks they probably have less THC to begin with. Don't do anything to the upper leaves and concentrate on the tied-down top flowers; after all of the flowers are harvested and cured, mix the various tops together. I agree with him. The fan leaves help the tops grow larger, so leave them alone.

Male Flowering and Producing Seeds

Because of the high cost of obtaining seeds, early on during his first year of growing Leo realized the necessity of growing his own seeds for future planting. He decided to only buy new seeds from unique varieties that he could experiment with. For the varieties he really liked, he decided to allow one male of each variety to flower in isolation from the rest of his plants.

After the male flowers opened, he held a piece of paper underneath the flowers and shook the pollen on it. Then he transferred the pollen to a small envelope, labeled it, and placed it in the freezer for future use. During the female flowering period, Leo selected a single flowering top from a particular plant that he temporarily isolated from the rest of them. He retrieved pollen from the same variety from his freezer and transferred the pollen to a small bowl. Using a watercolor brush, he "painted" the selected *cola* with the pollen, taking care that the pistils were thoroughly covered with it. Then he labeled the *cola* to ensure proper identification of the resulting seed. After leaving the plant alone for three or four days, he moved the pollinated plant back into the bloom room under the high-pressure sodium lights with the 12/12 cycle. Since the pollen was "stuck" on the pistils, the likelihood of it migrating to another flower was minimal, so Leo felt confident in moving another batch of mature plants from the outdoor urban garden to the flowering room.

By the time the new plants were in full flowering mode, the seeds from the pollinated *cola* were fully developed, and Leo harvested them by separating the seeds from the rest of the *cola* with his fingers. He placed the seeds in a small container, labeled it with the variety and date, and placed it in the freezer for the next growing cycle. If Leo had painted the

These pollen-producing staminate (male) flowers can help you forget the high cost of seed bank seeds.

Cannabis cuttings. These freshly cut cannabis stems and leaves will be dipped into a red rooting hormone gel and then placed in a sterile medium for rooting.

cola with the pollen of a different variety, he would have created an F1 hybrid. Avoid harvesting green seeds (they are infertile)— make sure the seeds have turned tan or mottled brown before harvesting them.

Cloning Around

The high cost of commercial marijuana seeds and the uncertainty of their essentially illegal acquisition have convinced many home growers to clone their favorite varieties to preserve their genetic traits. Leo decided to hedge his cannabis bets by producing both seeds and clones but soon discovered, as he put it, "clones are a pain in the ass." He was frustrated by their slow development, with less than half the growth rate of his plants sprouted from seed.

The root of the problem is, well, root development. Plants have two types of roots: those that are born from the embryo of the seed (*systemic roots*), and those that plants develop in order to reproduce asexually (*adventitious roots*). In nature, the adventitious roots are adventurous and take advantage of moist ground and a drooping stem touching it to grow and create a natural clone of the parent plant. But adventitious roots don't seem to have the vigor of systemic roots, and since root development is needed for foliage growth and subsequent flowering, clones take up space that can be utilized by faster-growing plants

and count in the total number of plants state law allows you.

That said, with patience, ruthlessness, and a couple of tricks, you can improve your success with clones. Generally speaking, the mother plant should be a favorite female that has been returned to vegetative growth after sex determination by changing the photoperiod back to long days and short nights, like 18/6. In other words, after you have culled all the males, put the females on a 12/12 cycle. But if you remove one female to another grow room and change the cycle to 18/6, flowering will cease and you can take cuttings to make clones. The plant should be healthy and vigorous, and I recommend lowering the nitrogen level of the mother by leaching the soil and not fertilizing her because plants with more carbohydrates and less nitrogen root the best.

Take cuttings from the lower branches, which have less nitrogen, using sterile razor blades and immediately place the cuttings in water. After taking all the cuttings you want, transfer them from water to peat cubes to root the cuttings. Leo used his fluorescents as the light source for the cuttings. Use liquid or gel rooting hormones rather than powders because the liquids and gels tend to adhere better to the cut stems. Just dip the cut end of the clone into the hormone gel and then into the hole in the rooting cube. Pinch to close the hole around the clone's stem. Some growers trim the clone's bottom leaves to reduce transpiration during the rooting process, and some even cut the top leaves in half. The humidity around the clones should be as high as possible, and the temperature around them should be 70 to 80 degrees Fahrenheit. Miniature "greenhouses" called *humidity domes* can house clones grown in dry climates and help them maintain a high humidity.

Clones that do not have any root formation after ten days should be discarded. As the clones develop roots, they can be moved to HID lights, but keep them at least two feet away from the bulbs at first because they're so sensitive. You can also transplant them to three-gallon pots with your usual growing medium and a weak, nitrogen-based fertilizer. From this point on, the clones will go through the usual vegetative cycle until you initiate flowering.

The Royal Flush

Flushing is flooding your containers with water several times and letting it drain out to remove any excessive fertilizers or salts deposited by the water used on the plants. That is the question home growers must answer before harvesting all their tops.

The flushers believe fertilizing should be suspended for two weeks before the harvest because excess nutrients may contribute to poor-tasting, hard-to-burn tops. When you stop fertilizing, they say, it forces the plants to use the nutrient reserves stored in its foliage. Plants that have been properly flushed have no harsh chemical or "green" taste from excess chlorophyll, nitrogen, and other elements in the final smoke. To properly flush the plants, water is poured through the soil, leaching out any remaining salts and fertilizers until it runs clear. Some flushers utilize cleansers for the soil known as *commercial flushing solutions*. Leo thinks they're a con—unnecessary and very expensive.

Nonflushing stoners can't detect the supposed "fertilizer-like taste." They not only think that it's really the magnesium in the chlorophyll that causes the "green" flavor, but they also believe that proper curing of the tops is the key to making them taste better and smoke more smoothly. Therefore, the tedious flushing process is unnecessary.

Leo takes a middle course, telling me that for the two weeks before the harvest, he gives the plants just water, which he calls "passive flushing." By this time, the plants have had all the fertilizer they are going to need. If I were ever going to grow marijuana again, I would use Leo's process.

By now, you have all-female plants in full bloom, and you've made the necessary preparations for future planting by producing seeds or clones, so it's time to begin the process of harvesting and preserving your crop.

CHAPTER 8

The Not-So-Grim Reaper

From Harvest to Storage

The harvest is probably the most fun time for the marijuana grower, but it also takes a lot of time to do it properly. In this chapter, I'll explain what trichomes are and why they're so important, provide a harvest timing checklist, and give you a list of equipment and tools you will need. Then I'll cover cutting, drying, and manicuring the tops, how to cure them, how to avoid problems, and finally how to store what you've harvested and cured.

When you're growing indoors, it can seem like the flowering lasts forever. You wait and wait until the tops are fully developed and ready to harvest, especially with some *sativa* varieties, which can take up to three months to fully ripen. *Indica* varieties take about half to two-thirds of that time. The relative ripeness of the flowering tops is indicated by two signals: the darkening of the pistils from white to reddish brown, and the swelling of the calyxes until they appear as if they are seeded. This swelling occurs gradually from the bottom of each flowering top to the tip of it, and depending on species and variety, takes about two weeks. This is the so-called *window of harvest* and theoretically the tops can be harvested any time this window is open. But since the THC amount is increasing and you have so much time invested in your plants already, it makes sense to wait until all the calyxes are swollen and the plant stalls in both flower development and vegetative growth before you start your harvest.

Trichomes: Key to Resin Production and Harvest Time

Glandular trichomes—also called (seriously!) resin heads—are hairs on the flower calyx that secrete aromatic THC-laden resins as long as the flowers remain unpollinated. The trichomes also are found on the bracts, leaves, and stems surrounding the flowers. By using a 30-power handheld microscope with a lamp (like stamp collectors use), you can monitor the progress of the trichomes throughout the

The glistening glandular trichomes produce the THC-containing resin in female flowers.

flowering cycle. The trichomes vary in resin production and color from variety to variety; most trichomes are clear and colorless, but some are amber-colored but still transparent.

The transparent nature of the trichomes is the key to resin production, and as long as they are clear, they are producing. But they also will let you know precisely when to harvest: when they lose their transparency and become first translucent and then milky white. The trichomes start withering at this point and the pistils turn from white to brown, indicating that flowering is essentially over. Start checking your plants after a month of blooming to monitor their progress. The best time to harvest is when about half of the trichomes are clear and the rest are turning white.

Some experts give other estimates, and it can get quite confusing, but I don't think it matters that much. Just harvest within the window and don't wait too long. Try to avoid the temptation to smoke some, because you'll just be drying them in a microwave (a grave sin in the world of medical marijuana), and you won't have time to cure them properly. Just be patient, do the job well, and know that

When these trichomes turn from clear to cloudy, flowering is ending.

the tops will probably be excellent. After all, they have been engineered by breeders to be the finest *sinsemilla* at the peak of its potency.

I've heard that taking samples of the tops during the harvest window will tell you when your plants are at their peak of THC production, but this is absurd. First, you're going to destroy the symmetry of these nicely shaped tops, and, as we shall see, the drying and curing process takes some time. Second, can you really detect the subtle changes in THC levels that the plant is going through? I don't think so—no more than you could detect the difference between a beer with 6 percent alcohol and one with 8 percent. Short of a lab test, you're just guessing because the effects of marijuana on the brain vary from variety to variety and from person to person. Your perception of the strength of the high is also altered by your mental state combined with the circumstances of the setting at the time of the test. In other words, a test like that is too subjective, so just watch the plant's development and use your best judgment about the moment the harvest should begin.

Equipment and Tools for the Harvest

You should approach your first harvest with some care because the plants are more often destroyed by improper handling than anything else. Before you begin cutting and trimming, remember that the less you handle the floral clusters, the better they will look and

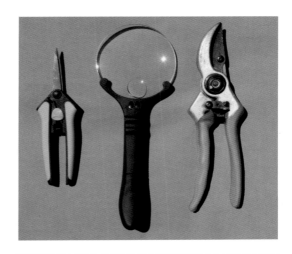

Tools needed for the harvesting and subsequent trimming of the tops: spring-loaded scissors, magnifying glass, and pruning shears.

taste. So try to handle only the stem ends of the tops you trim. No matter the size or condition of your plants, when you have determined it's time to harvest, you're about to make a big mess, so it's a good idea to prepare for it by having certain items on hand:

- A glass-topped table and comfortable chair. These are available from stores selling patio furniture. You will have leaves, stems, flower tops, and resin everywhere, so you'll need a table with a glass top, ideally, or one covered with aluminum foil to catch any trichomes that might fall off the plants as you process them. You will be doing a lot of scissor work, so a comfortable chair is a necessity.

- A drying rack or food dehydrator. Food dehydrators are available at kitchen shops. As you remove the tops from the stems, you will need a drying rack of some sort to hang them on—perhaps a small clothesline in a closet. If you live in a climate with high humidity, a food dehydrator may work better and faster than a clothesline.

- A **drying screen for leaves and the smaller tops.** A window screen will work fine.

- A **collection of simple tools—pruning shears, scissors, and gloves.** You'll need pruning shears for the larger stems, like the pruners commonly sold in hardware stores and gardening shops, and small, sharp scissors with comfortable handles for trimming and manicuring; both the pruners and the scissors range widely in price. Spring-loaded pruners and scissors make the job a little easier if you face hours of pruning and trimming, which may be the case if you're harvesting twelve large *sativa* plants. Some growers wear latex or thin plastic gloves; they'll eventually become covered with a thin film of resin. This is proto-hashish, so many growers dutifully scrape the resin off the gloves and smoke it. Leo notes that since he will soon have ounces of smokable tops, he's not going to become a "lowly resin-scraper."

Leo carefully trims the top to remove as many of the chlorophyll-laden leaves as possible.

THE HARVEST CHECKLIST

You can begin harvesting your plants if any of these conditions occur:

- The pistils begin turning color from white to reddish-brown.

- The trichomes change from transparent to milky white.

- The calyxes begin to swell.

- You need to smoke or otherwise ingest medical marijuana because your supply is exhausted.

- Your plants face a serious threat from pests like spider mites.

The Cannabis Beauty Shop: Cutting, Drying, and Manicuring

There are basically two avenues to approaching the harvest: harvesting the flower tops individually as they mature or cutting down the entire plant and processing all the tops. Before you chop down your first plant, give some thought to the concept of the total surface area of your finished tops. The more you break them down to a manageable size, the more surface area they will have, meaning that they will dry and cure much faster. The important point about drying is patience, because the preliminary drying is just the start of the curing process to remove all the chlorophyll you can from the tops you harvest. (I'll explain why below.) You don't want to remove all the moisture, just a large percentage of it. So start by not watering your plants at all for a full day before cutting them down.

Leo's midget, autoflowering varieties are less than three feet tall and have small stems, so after trimming off the large fan leaves, he just hangs the entire plant on a clothesline in a closet to dry. But this won't work with his eight-foot-tall *sativa* giants, because if he hangs the whole plant up, it will take too much time to dry. The water in the plant will have to pass through the surfaces of the leaves and tops. Besides, he doesn't have the room to hang up those huge plants. So his first step with those plants is to reduce the tops to a manageable size by cutting off the branches from the main stems. Generally speaking, if your plants are larger than three feet tall, you should not hang the whole plant but rather cut it apart to make smaller units to hang up to dry.

After you have cut the large branches from the main stem, the next step is to cut the flowering tops off those branches. Although one giant, cured *cola* is extremely impressive to show off to tight-lipped friends, it will take much longer to dry and cure—and it is actually impractical. I suggest carefully breaking it down to smaller units with more surface area. After all, you're not going to be selling it; you're going to be smoking it. Other drawbacks to

If the tops are too small to hang on a string to dry, use a drying screen.

large *colas* include a large stem that will be difficult to dry, the whole top will be more prone to mold, and tops that size are hard to store properly.

Since no one smokes the stems, why keep them? Leo cuts the smaller tops (which have little stems of their own) off the branches to make "nugget-sized" tops. This way, the total surface area of the nuggets will be many times the surface area of the unprocessed plant. At this point in the process, you are separating the tops from the stems and have not yet started trimming or "manicuring" the tops.

After the tops are separated from the stems, you want to remove as much leaf material as possible. Why? The leaf material contains much more chlorophyll than the resin-laden tops, and it's much more difficult to cure. All the larger leaves (not the fan leaves—you already removed them after they turned yellow) should be cut from the tops first and placed in a container for the low-THC trim. This material makes for lousy smoking, but it can be used in cooking, as we shall see in chapter 10. Next, as you are breaking down the larger tops into nuggets, you will encounter single-bladed leaves sticking out of the tops, many coated with resin.

At this point, there is a minor debate, because some growers believe that these leaves act as a wrapper to protect the floral clusters and should be left on. Leo and I disagree, because those little leaves are resin-coated

and no smoker wants to take on the tedious job of cutting out those tiny leaves from a compact bud.

They just want to smoke it. For Leo, the manicuring takes place in two stages: before drying and before curing. The first manicuring takes place on the branches cut from the main stems, and Leo does what he calls a basic trim, cutting off the leaves from the larger tops and placing them in a separate container that he labels "Bud Leaves." They are more smokable than the first set of low-THC leaves, but most marijuana connoisseurs only use the leaves for cooking. He notes that for his setup, it's easier for him to hang the branches (without leaves and just with the flowers) for drying than to hang nugget-size tops. For our purposes here, I don't separate the leaves into two containers—it's all trim to me and will be used in cooking.

During the manicuring process, huge tops, like the 'Chemo Iranian' top shown here, should be broken down to smaller units for ease in handling and curing.

To summarize the process, here are the steps that Leo takes to dry the flowering tops on his larger plants before curing:

1. Process one plant at a time, or you will be overwhelmed.

2. Cut off all the large leaves and place them in a paper bag or box labeled "Trim."

3. Remove all the branches from the main stem and discard the stem.

4. Remove any medium-size leaves from around the flower clusters, but do not try to remove the very small leaves that are close to the flowers. Place the medium-size leaves in the trim bag or in another bag labeled "Better Trim."

5. Separate the flowering tops into smaller, nugget-size units 1 to 3 inches long and $1/2$ to 1 inch wide. Place them on a screen or screens to dry in a closet.

6. On a daily basis, monitor the resistance of the little stems on the nuggets to bending. When they resist bending and seem ready to snap, they have dried enough.

Manicuring the Tops

Manicuring, the very close trimming of the tops either before or after drying, is optional. Originally, in the world of clandestine growing before marijuana was legalized for medical use, the purpose of manicuring was cosmetic because it made the tops more beautiful in the eyes of the buyer and hence more profitable to the grower. In the world of state-legalized marijuana growing for personal use, it is not necessary.

That said, some home growers still manicure their tops. Manicuring can be arduous and often results in hand cramps, and that's why enterprising inventors have devised numerous mechanical trimming devices, like the TrimPro Trimbox. I've seen a demonstration of this device, and it works very well. All you do is take a branch of a freshly harvested plant in your hand and move it over the grate with a back-and-forth motion while rotating the plant at the same time. It retails for about $900. Leo snorts in derision at this "fancy equipment," noting that "a pro can trim a pound in a day by hand"—that is, if you have

that much and want to devote an entire day to doing what a machine can do in an hour.

Manicuring each of your nugget-size tops by hand takes concentration and careful work as you use scissors to meticulously trim away any leaves or leaf remnants until you are left with only the resin-coated flowers.

Curing the Tops

If drying is merely a physical process, then curing is an art—much like cooking and gardening are at times. Curing marijuana is essentially the fine-tuning of temperature and humidity to degrade the chlorophyll—the "green" flavor stoners despise—and transform it into carotene and xanthophylls, which are more pleasant to taste. If this is sounding vaguely familiar, think of fall foliage—it's the same process, only controlled and regulated by the grower, not nature.

Besides the chlorophyll contained in the flowering tops, there are other chemicals that change as well. In lay language, the fruits (yes, the tops are fruits because they usually contain seeds) are still ripening, and as long as you don't dry them out too quickly and leave unprocessed chlorophyll in them, the green flavor will vanish over time—the process can last two months or more for "advanced curing."

Here are the steps to cure the nugget-size tops you have dried:

1. Select a curing container. It should be opaque because ultraviolet light can degrade the tops and bleach them. I recommend the ceramic canisters used to store coffee beans. They have a hinged lid with a clamp and rubber seal that works perfectly to retain some moisture inside.

2. Place the dried tops from your screens loosely in the canisters. Do not pack them in the canisters.

3. Over a few weeks, the small amount of moisture left in the tops will help cure them by transforming the chlorophyll.

4. Open each canister every day to admit fresh oxygen and check for any signs of mold on the tops.

5. Once a week, remove a small top and smoke it to check for flavor and smoothness. When the flavor is not "green" and the smoke is not so harsh that it makes you cough, the curing process is complete.

Storing Your Cannabis

During his first season, Leo reported that he grew six primary varieties and three experimental varieties. He had a total of sixteen plants that came and went (never more than twelve at one time), and the total dry weight of flowering tops (not including trim) came to 1.5 pounds.

"I grew too much," he confided to me. "Now I'm violating the state medical marijuana statute for possession of what I grew. And I'm not allowed to sell it or give it away. So I have to throw some of it away, or hide it." Leo estimated that his larder would last him two years because he smokes an average of one ounce per month to help with his back pain. In the end, he couldn't bear to throw it away, so he stored it.

The THC in the cured tops naturally degrades into *CBD*, which is nonpsychoactive cannabidiol. That process is aggravated by the two biggest enemies of cured marijuana: light and heat. Ideally, if I were a grower and could choose the best preservation method for marijuana, I would vacuum-seal the totally cured tops and then irradiate them with the same process used for food. This would kill all bacteria and mold spores. Next, I would place them in a light-impervious container, and store it in the back of the refrigerator. But, unfortunately, home irradiators are not yet available to consumers. However, if you omit the irradiation, this method still works very well. Refrigeration retards the breakdown of THC, but whatever container you use must be airtight. You can freeze the seeds but not the tops.

In addition to light and heat, another enemy of cured marijuana is dryness—poorly stored tops dry out, lose potency, and fall apart.

Use opaque canisters for curing instead of transparent jars like these, unless you store them in the dark, since the ambient light can hurt the cured tops.

Leo prefers the canister-style jar with the easily closed top and rubber ring to prevent outside air from entering during the curing process. The tops at left are 'Lowryder #2'.

There are commercial storage containers available, like Tightpac and Tightvac from the same company, and CannaFresh jars that come in various sizes. But some of these containers are plastic, which most growers don't like because it leaches and imparts a chemical odor to the marijuana. The real drawback with polyurethane containers, and especially thin plastic bags, is not the supposed chemical odor, but rather the fact that they are porous to air and may cause the tops to dry out. In the refrigerator, with a humidity of about 65 percent, the bags are also porous to water vapor, so your tops may rehydrate, making them unsmokable.

Some storage containers are transparent because they are used to display tops in a dispensary setting, thus admitting THC-destroying light. Some of these are made of glass and could easily break if dropped. And some are quite expensive, so you could also shop secondhand stores in order to find inexpensive, opaque ceramic cannabis canisters for both curing and storage. Leo packs the canisters so the tops don't rub against each other and lose dried trichomes, but he doesn't pack them so tightly that they are crushed. These canisters are airtight, very difficult to break, and store easily in the refrigerator. I use the same ones for storing coffee beans.

You have learned how to harvest your tops, break them down into a manageable size, dry them, and cure them, so you now should have enough marijuana to ease whatever medical conditions you are growing it for—assuming, of course, that you have not run into any pests or problems that would jeopardize your crop. But if you do run into problems, the next chapter will help you troubleshoot them.

CHAPTER 9

Patience, Pestilence, and Panaceas

Dealing with Problems

As tough as the cannabis weed seems to be, remember that it's in captivity now—subdued, domesticated, and confined to an unnatural environment. Leo essentially is raising twelve houseplants—psychoactive ones to be sure—but those now-delicate plants are susceptible to dangers indoors that they would not face if they had been born free in the foothills of the Hindu Kush. Some of the creatures threatening Leo's babies are barely visible to the human eye, but before we break out the magnifying glass, let's look at the bigger picture: the health of that herbaceous, woody annual that you are growing.

The Problem: Overwatering

THE SYMPTOMS: Leaves curled down and yellowed; the top layer of soil is constantly wet, fungal growth, slow growth.

THE SOLUTION: If the saucers under the pots still have water standing in them, the plants shouldn't be watered. Water standing on the roots of marijuana prevents oxygen from reaching them, so the plants will suffocate. Let the plants dry out a bit between waterings and they'll be fine. In my basement growing operation, I didn't have saucers under the large tomato cans I was using as pots; rather, the water simply drained out of the cans' holes and was collected in containers under the growing bench. Thus there was no way that the roots could be flooded. A final test is to poke your finger into the potting soil. If the soil is wet by the first joint down, don't water. That's a finger joint I'm referring to.

The Problem: Overfertilizing

THE SYMPTOMS: Leaves that turn brown or look burned. Although stunted, weak-looking plants may signal that you're not giving them enough nitrogen, this rarely happens with novice growers who tend to overfertilize. Remember that nitrogen produces leaves. In chile peppers, excess nitrogen means lots of leaves and no pods. It's the same with flowering marijuana tops—when they're ready to reproduce and flowering commences, the plants don't need any more nitrogen, so it makes no sense to pamper the plants and feed them all the time. See the section on fertilizing in chapter 6.

THE SOLUTION: Flush the containers and stop any fertilizing until normal growth returns.

The Problem: Flies, Mites, and Aphids

THE SYMPTOMS: Yellowing leaves; tiny, white flying insects (whiteflies); webs on the bottoms of leaves or the flowering tops (spider mites); wilting plants (aphids).

THE SOLUTION: I'm going to show you how to fight and conquer the indoor and outdoor pests that frantically want to molest your fast-maturing females with their flowering tops, so the most important thing first: Leo and I prefer mechanical solutions over chemical ones. The most commonly encountered indoor growing pests are whiteflies, spider mites, and aphids. They are all vegetarian vampires and they want to suck the life out of your plants. Indoor infestations are the worst, because the pests won't have the natural predators that they would outdoors.

Whiteflies look harmless enough, but they will do major damage to your pet plants.

WHITE FLIES: Whiteflies are harmful because they suck juices from plants, causing the leaves to shrivel, turn yellow, and drop. They can carry viruses as well. They fly from one plant to another, carrying disease with them, and quickly attack all of the plants in your indoor garden. These pests are white and about $1/16$ inch long. Adult and young whiteflies feed on the underside of leaves. Organic insecticides have only a limited effect on whiteflies, as they quickly build up resistance to them, and most are not very effective in garden situations. Insecticidal soaps and oils are only marginally effective. Physical removal of the flies is the best solution. You should move infested indoor plants to the outside, lay them on their sides, and use the garden hose to spray the underside of the leaves to physically remove the flies and their nymphs. In the grow room or bloom room, hang flypaper ribbons without insecticide and trap the flies.

The leaves to the immediate right and left of the flowering top show spider mite damage from those little suckers underneath the leaves.

SPIDER MITES: I despise spider mites more than any other pest because they are insidious. Under optimal conditions (about 80 degrees Fahrenheit), the two-spotted spider mite can hatch from an egg in as little as three days and become sexually mature in as little as five days. One female can lay up to twenty eggs per day and can live for two to four weeks, laying hundreds of eggs. A single mature female can spawn a population of a million mites in a month or less. Spider mites look like tiny moving red dots and are almost too small to be seen with the naked eye; however, they are easily seen with a 10-power hand lens. Adult females rarely exceed half a millimeter (.02 inches) in length. Spider mites live in colonies, mostly on the undersurfaces of leaves; a single colony may contain hundreds of individuals. The name "spider mite" comes from the silk webbing most species produce on infested leaves. The presence of webbing

is an easy way to distinguish them from all other types of mites. So, spot the webs, not the mites. The webs reflect light, so turn off your grow lights and use a narrow-beam flashlight and a magnifying glass to inspect the plants. Look beneath the lower, large fan leaves first, because those are the most vulnerable to early mite infestations.

Mites cause damage by sucking cell contents from leaves and tops. At first, the damage shows up as a stippling of light dots on the tops of the leaves; sometimes the leaves take on a bronze color. As the feeding continues, the leaves turn yellow and drop off. Often leaves, twigs, and fruit are covered with large amounts of webbing. Damage is usually worse when compounded by water stress. They can kill the plant if left uncontrolled.

Miticides are not recommended for controlling spider mites because they will be inhaled with the smoke of any tops or leaves that you smoke. In their early stages, spider mites can be eliminated by washing the plants with a mild soap solution, then spraying the plant with water, including the undersides of leaves where the mites usually harbor. Repeat this process every three or four days until the mites are gone. If spider mites attack the plants in your bloom room and you don't want to subject the tops to water spraying that might damage or destroy trichomes, your only solution is to harvest all the plants immediately.

APHIDS: Aphids are usually brown or light green and soft-bodied. They cluster on leaf undersides or on stems sucking plant juices and excreting a sticky liquid called *honeydew*, which creates spots on the foliage. A black fungus called sooty mold may then grow on the honeydew. Severe infestations can cause wilting, stunting, curling, and leaf distortion. Normally aphid predators such as lady bird beetles (ladybugs) and their larvae (black and orange segmented creatures about $\frac{1}{8}$ inch long) keep the aphid numbers low, but the aphids can multiply quickly. Spray the aphids with soapy water and then rinse them away as a mechanical means of removal.

When left untreated, gangs of aphids can devastate your crop.

This copper-phobic, beeraholic snail is much tougher than it looks.

The Problem: Heavy Pest Infestation Beyond Mechanical Removal

THE SYMPTOMS: Webs totally covering your flowering tops (spider mites); clouds of whiteflies; aphids so thick that the plants are dying.

THE SOLUTION: It's inconvenient to constantly wash your plants, but it is an inconvenience you must occasionally put up with. Remember, the earlier you catch the infestation, the easier the treatment will be. Leo, who was inexperienced in recognizing the early signs of spider mites, had such a severe attack on three nearly mature plants in his bloom room that he had no choice but to harvest immediately. After removing infested plants, many growers opt for fumigation of the room to kill any lingering pests. I have used this technique in my winter greenhouse and discovered that Raid Flying Insect Killer is particularly effective—especially for whiteflies and aphids. I've never found any insecticide effective against spider mites, although neem oil, made from the neem tree, seems to be an effective treatment for repelling, rather than immediately killing, the pests. The oil is nontoxic to humans and pets, and should be diluted with water and an emulsifier like soap before being sprayed on infested plants. Neem oil spray, however, may alter the taste of the marijuana tops.

The Problem: Snails and Slugs

THE SYMPTOMS: Plants chopped down; slimy trails all over the outdoor garden.

THE SOLUTION: I've eaten snails, and that's the way I prefer them: on my plate rather than on my garden plants. Leo feels the same way and related the story of a grower friend who innocently placed his indoor plants in the late-spring garden in his backyard. The friend moved six young plants barely six inches tall into the yard in small pots, intending to transplant them the next day. But when he went out to take on that task, all that was left of the plants was the stub of a stem—and the slimy trails left by snails. This will not happen in the indoor garden, but snail or slug damage is a problem outdoors.

These pests can be controlled, of course, but don't poison them. Snail and slug bait containing metaldehyde or methiocarb have killed countless thousands of domestic pets and birds as well as beneficial insects and earthworms. Iron phosphate is considered to be a "safe bait,"

CLEANING UP THE MESS

Suppose you face Leo's biggest crisis: mature flowering tops so infested with spider mites during indoor flowering that they must be harvested immediately. You know you don't want to smoke mites and their webs, which will cover your tops after you harvest, but how do you remove them? First, don't worry about damage to the tops—that's already happened and you're in the salvage mode called "save what you can." If you're a grower with a phobia about simply spraying off your infested fresh tops with a blast of water, your options for cleaning the webs off the tops are limited to USB Mini Vacuum Cleaners designed to clean your keyboard, dust-removal sprays, and Q-tips. Whichever you use, remember to clean the tops when they are freshly harvested, not dried, because the fresh tops are tougher and can withstand the physical abuse you're about to subject them to.

Most of the USB cleaners sold have very low ratings by buyers on websites, so you'd have to buy a Metro Vacuum ED500, a 500-watt, expensive sucker (MSRP $82.50) that may have too much power; that said, you can adjust the distance and therefore the power of the sucking. Dust-removal sprays do the opposite, blow the webs and mites off the plants—do this outside to avoid contaminating your grow room. If you place a thin tube into the air outlet slot, you can carefully direct and focus the application of the spray. Q-tips take time to use on the webs, but by twirling them and running them across the tops, you can remove most of the mite damage and loosen the rest for air-spraying or vacuuming. Be sure to dispose of the Q-tips in the usual manner—by fire.

After you have cleaned your tops to the best of your ability, proceed with the drying and curing procedures discussed in chapter 8. If you were diligent with your web work, by the time the cleaning is completed, all evidence of the mites and webs will be gone. The resulting healing smoke should relieve all your symptoms, including excessive worrying. *Indica* varieties are particularly good for eliminating worry.

After you've saved the crop and stopped worrying, you must disinfect your grow room or bloom room. Remove all your equipment to the backyard (assuming it's not raining), including your grow benches and the pots the plants were in. Mix a mild bleach solution and spray down every surface of the room. Then, using clean rags or paper towels, wipe everything up. Dispose of the wipes in your grow trash—not in your usual household trash—they'll be too wet to burn. People living in urban areas—or in rural areas where burning is prohibited—could put the wipes in the household trash. Remove the dirt from the pots and throw it away with your grow trash, and use the bleach spray to disinfect them. By dipping rags into the bleach solution, and then squeezing out as much moisture as you can, you can now carefully wipe down all your equipment and the benches. Reinstall these in your grow room or bloom room, and you're ready to restart the cycle.

but I have an aversion to spreading any kind of poison. Leo shudders at the thought, so it's another reason for building an urban garden that's a barrier against them. It's much better to creatively deter snails and slugs

BARRIERS, TRAPS, AND OTHER TECHNIQUES: Snails and slugs are copper-phobic—the slime of snails and slugs reacts with copper and this repels them. You can create barriers around your plants with scrap copper, or buy self-adhesive copper tape to wrap around the rims of the pots. These copper-phobic mollusks are also beeraholics—I'm not kidding. If you place beer in a shallow dish, you can trap them easily and recycle them if they're not eaten first by starlings, which love them marinated in Miller Lite. Some master gardeners recommend an ingenious solution of spraying weeds with beer so the snails will eat them. Also, try planting "repellent" species—like lavender, thyme, sage, mint, and geraniums—that the slugs and snails hate.

Rough mulch can also be an effective barrier, so even if the plants are in pots, surround them with crushed eggshells, pine needles, straw, or the bark sold in garden stores for mulching. While you're doing that, you can make simple traps in the yard, such as upside down plant pots and wooden boards where snails and slugs hide and breed. Also, check regularly under rocks, logs, and any thick vegetation you have in your garden. If you find any and don't want to touch them, use tongs to throw them into a bucket of soapy water, where they will be unable to climb out and soon drown. You can just recycle the dead pests into the compost pile. Since snails and slugs are most active at night and like moisture, water in the morning so the top of the ground will dry out by evening; dry ground will harbor fewer of these mollusks.

Finally, introduce some slug predators into your yard. A surprising number of domesticated animals eat them, including dogs, cats, ducks, and chickens, so they would be likely candidates for controlling the slimy ones. Just one note of caution—ducks and chickens eat vegetation, too. My friend Harald Zoschke, a chile grower who lives in southwestern Germany, reports that a slug predator has moved into his yard, built a nest under his gas grill out of bamboo leaves, and is eating every slug he can find. It's a European hedgehog (*Erinaceus europaeus*) he named Schneckenfresser ("slug-eater"). Leo tells me his beloved pet, an ornate box turtle (*Terrapene ornata*) that lives in his backyard, just loves snails. "I watched François in awe," he said, "he couldn't use a snail fork, so he just grabbed a big snail with his front claws and gently extracted the good part with his beak. He's part French, like me."

The Problem: Fungi

THE SYMPTOMS: Powdery, white or gray growth on leaves and tops (*Botrytis*), and wilting (root rot).

THE SOLUTION: We saw in chapter 5 that a fungus causes the damping-off of marijuana seedlings, and this is usually the result of excessive humidity in the germination room. Growers living in climates with high humidity have another problem—mold—which can quickly ruin a crop either indoors or out. Particularly troublesome is *Botrytis*, also known as gray mold or bud mold. *Botrytis* attacks the entire plant (except the roots) but seems to favor the flowering tops and can turn them into a gray powder in a matter of seven to ten days if left alone. Don't even think about using fungicides; instead, solve the problem mechanically. First, take care that your growing areas are clear of all debris and make sure your light intensity is as high as you can make it, including buying new bulbs if yours are more than a year old and are constantly used. Check your ventilation

system and increase the air circulation by adding more fans and installing a dehumidifier. All you have to do is bring the humidity in your grow room or bloom room to below 50 percent, and that will prevent the fungus from growing and spreading by releasing spores.

Root rot (*Phytophthora*) is caused by spores growing on water-saturated roots. To counter this, make sure all plant growing media drains well and that container plants don't sit in saucers full of water.

If you find mold on any of your live plants, be ruthless. Cut off all infected parts and destroy them by burning them in your fireplace, barbecue unit, or the firepit in your backyard. In addition to *Botrytis*, other molds can attack your plants, such as downy mildew and powdery mildew. The prevention is the same: cleanliness, air circulation, good ventilation, and humidity reduced to below 50 percent.

The Problem: Weather Damage Outdoors

THE SYMPTOMS: Missing or damaged leaves, blown-over plants.

THE SOLUTION: Of all the problems that could occur with marijuana grown outdoors, the worst are weather-related, including high winds and downpours from storms, hail that can strip the tops and leaves from your plants, and late frosts in the spring and early ones in

If marijuana can thrive in a harsh environment like this, there's absolutely no reason you can't grow it successfully.

the fall. Weather problems give you even more reasons for growing outdoors in containers. If a storm threatens or a frost is predicted, you can bring your plants indoors temporarily until the danger is past.

The Problem: Other Pest Damage Outdoors

THE SYMPTOMS: Chewed or shredded leaves, the same symptoms for insect pests.

THE SOLUTION: The good news is that less than 1 percent of the millions of different insect species are considered to be serious pests. The bad news is that leaves hundreds of bad ones that you might have to worry about. That said, many of these pests attack humans and other animals rather than plants—mosquitos, flies, ticks, and bedbugs, for example. It is my experience that although all the indoor pests—including whiteflies, aphids, and spider mites—can attack your plants outdoors, such assaults are less frequent in the open environment of your backyard where there's good air circulation, strong light, and many other plant species to attack—many far more vulnerable than tough cannabis.

Yes, deer could attack your plants if they have nothing else to eat. But if you live in a city or town and have a fenced or walled yard, this will be unlikely if they can't see the plants to begin with. You can always use cheap chicken wire to further extend the height of your fence or wall so that even the hungriest Olympic buck will not be able to jump it. And sure, groundhogs, moles, and other subterranean mammals could chew the roots off your plants, but not if you're growing in containers. And yes, it's possible that a swarm of grasshoppers could descend on your plants and reduce them to stubble in a few minutes, or a squadron of Japanese beetles could get the munchies for your flowering tops and have a nice, very relaxing lunch at your expense. But if you offer your plants physical protection, this won't happen.

OUTDOOR PROTECTION OPTIONS: Leo's urban garden raised bed has an arched cover that guards against most insects, especially large ones. Other growers use fine-mesh netting over individual plants to fend off grasshoppers, leafhoppers, and beetles. These are by far the best solutions. Spraying a mist of insecticide on a two-inch, mature, and hungry grasshopper would be like fighting off Godzilla with a garden hose.

In Yucatán and other tropical regions, growers use screenhouses. Think greenhouse with the sides and roofs made with screening rather than glass or fiberglass, just like the way swimming pools are enclosed in Florida and other mosquito-infested areas. In many ways, screenhouses are better than greenhouses. First, because of constant exposure to the sun and breezes and even rain, screenhouses don't create an artificial environment for your plants; rather, they duplicate the same environment as the backyard, but with physical protection. If you're worried about rain dripping on your trichomes, which of course happens often to plants being cultivated

The habanero chiles in this Yucatán screenhouse are well protected from wind and insect pests.

outdoors, you can always cover the top screen with a tarp when rain threatens and remove it when the sun returns after the storm. Second, the physical protection of a screenhouse also means that the worst pests—spider mites, aphids, and whiteflies—are much less likely to attack your plants. But if they do, ladybugs, can be confined in the screenhouse until they eat all the pests and then can be released to nature after their work is done. Compared to other insects, ladybugs live a surprisingly long life as adults—three to nine months—so free them after their captivity so they can continue their life cycle. As mentioned before, ladybug larvae can be even more effective for pest control than mature ladybugs.

If you're handy with tools, you could build (in sections) a small version of the screenhouse pictured above for summer growing, and then take it down and store it after the season ends. Be sure to use screening like PureView from Milgard that has greater openness (74 percent versus standard screen at 59 percent), allowing more light to enter the screenhouse and greater airflow for better ventilation.

With any luck, you will not have any of these problems, or if you do, you can solve them without losing your crop. If this is the case, we've seen in chapter 8 that you now have stored your manicured and cured tops in their containers, and the trim in others. I'm not going to explain how to smoke marijuana, but for people who can't or won't smoke it, the next chapter tells you how to cook with it.

Ladybugs can help you eliminate pests in your marijuana garden.

CHAPTER 10

Cannabis Cooking

With Dosages and Recipes

One of the biggest challenges of cooking with cannabis is determining the right dosage so you do not have an adverse reaction from becoming too stoned—like paranoia, panic, and anxiety. In the chapter to follow, I cover safe THC dosages along with suggestions for dosing in cooking, and then I explain how to transform the trim for easy use in recipes. Finally, I've included recipes for the simplest and easiest things to make: drinks, snacks, baked goodies, cookies, and candies.

In his 1860 book, *The Seven Sisters of Sleep: Popular History of the Seven Prevailing Narcotics of the World*, Mordecai Cubitt Cooke surveyed the use of cannabis products in cooking. The dried tops, he discovered, were "boiled in fat, butter, or oil, with a little water; the filtered product is employed in all kinds of pastry. Made into an electuary [medicinal paste] with dates or figs and honey. This preparation is of a dark brown or almost black colour . . . with the addition of spices, cloves, cinnamon, pepper, amber, and musk, the preparation is used as an aphrodisiac. The confection most in use among the Arabs is called Dawamese. This is mingled with other stimulating substances, so as to administer to the sensual gratifications, which appear to be the *summum bonum* of oriental existence."

So, from the very beginning of cannabis cookery, the most popular recipes were those for snacks and sweet treats. And this fondness has not changed for centuries, if not millennia. Those types of foods are the best THC delivery system because they contain small doses that can help you manage the total dosage you are striving for to relieve your symptoms.

Safe THC Dosages

When the Canadian Consortium for the Investigation of Cannabinoids released studies of THC testing of marijuana plant parts, it noted, "With regards to the dried cannabis, the THC content varies based on the part of the plant it contains: 10–12% in flowers, 1–2% in leaves, 0.1–0.3% in stalks." These figures were corroborated by a Japanese study, stating that 1.5 percent of THC was found in the leaves. Since there are no accurate and inexpensive home kits for THC testing, I have developed a method to approximate dosages based on these figures and the method of cooking recommended below. If you don't know the strength of the particular variety you are growing, look it up on BudGenius.com. I assume that they use the same methodology as the Werc Shop—namely, expressing the percentage of THC in milligrams to grams of the marijuana tested, and then converting that to a percentage.

In an experiment with a commercial cookie mix to test the efficacy of trim, Leo used 'Super Lemon Haze' with good, controllable results. BudGenius indicates that the THC percentage levels from two separate tests of 'Super Lemon Haze' from different growers were 17.14 and 20.48, for an average of 18.81. Using the leaf statistics above, multiply 18.81 by 13.6 percent (flower versus leaf from the Canadian study), and that will give you an approximate leaf THC percentage for Leo's variety of 2.5 percent. That's higher than average, but 'Super Lemon Haze' is strong, as smokers know. Now, not all of the THC in the leaves will be extracted in the butter and oil procedures explained on the following pages, but at least this gives you a benchmark. Then, by proceeding to use the butter or oil in cooking, and then gauging the effect on your body and mind from one sample, you will be able to dose yourself with some degree of accuracy. One final comment: If you run out of trim and still want to cook, then use the tops, but in this case, reduce the amount you use by 86.4 percent, resulting in using a mere 3.8 grams in the butter or oil procedures.

The Transformation of the Trim

I should note that a familiar and warm setting is particularly important with orally consumed marijuana, because if you eat too many of, say, the delicious cookies in this chapter, your experience can resemble that of taking a psychedelic drug rather than merely smoking some marijuana. I did some minor experimentation with psychedelics when I was in my twenties, and in every instance the setting—including the physical surroundings, the other people around, the music, and even the food served—became a very important part of the experience. I gave up psychedelics because invariably I had to become the "trip director" when someone couldn't handle the experience. This is precisely what I'm trying to avoid by moderating the dosage through the techniques described later in this chapter.

Now you have three grades of cannabis to play with—or rather, treat yourself with. The tops are the highest grade, of course, so those will probably be the only part of the plant you will smoke. But then you have two grades of trim from the harvest: the low-THC bag and the "bud leaves," as Leo calls them. There is no way known to remove all the chlorophyll from the bud leaves without destroying the THC, so neither the bud leaves nor the trim will taste great when smoked. The leaves manicured from the harvested tops could be blended with some of the cured tops to extend and dilute them, but purists will shudder and shake their heads as they read this.

Leo and I finally agree on something: the best use for the trim is in preparing and cooking the recipes in this chapter. We also agree that the way I used to cook with marijuana— just straining some and adding it haphazardly to boxed brownie mix without even measuring it—is old hat and a bit dangerous. Nowadays, marijuana is not added directly to the food being cooked, but rather to the cooking ingredients themselves, namely butter, vegetable oil, and baking "flour." Recipes for making these are included here. And since you'll be using trim, not tops, you can better regulate the dosage of the THC being ingested and avoid tripping your eyeballs out from foods that are simply too potent. But first, the trim must be processed into the basic cooking ingredients used in the recipes.

The Basic Cannabis Cooking Ingredients

I've kept this as simple as possible by using the trim to make butter for sautéeing and baking, oil for frying, and flour for baking.

Like the capsaicin in chile peppers, THC is not miscible with water, but it is with fats, oils, and alcohol. So the goal is to extract as much of the THC as possible from the trim without cooking it at too high a temperature or for too long, which can degrade the THC.

The finished, THC-enhanced cooking ingredients are then used in the preparation of just about any recipe. But I recommend making snacks, cookies, and other dishes that have small, discrete servings to make it easier to adjust the dosage. Remember that as with curing the tops, the total surface area of the particles will be important. The finer the particle used in the extractions, the better the THC extraction of the butter or oil will be.

Compounded Butter

Compound butters are simply butters infused with other ingredients like herbs or garlic, so marijuana fits right in with that concept. But instead of creaming all the ingredients together, the butter needs to be heated to extract the THC. For the extraction apparatus, Leo used a double boiler that could not get the butter any hotter than 212°F, so the risk of degrading the THC was quite low. A slow cooker set to low and covered would also work well.

The butter will be faintly green and have a pleasant, herbal aroma. Leo covered his with foil, marked it with a warning label with a "radioactive" symbol, and stored it in the refrigerator. It will keep there for up to a month.

1 ounce dried low-THC trim
1 pound butter

1. Pulverize the trim in a spice mill. Cut the butter into chunks, place it in the top of a double boiler, and turn up the heat to high. When the butter has melted and is hot—about 10 minutes—add the pulverized trim and stir.

2. Let the marijuana steep in the butter, stirring occasionally. After about 20 minutes, turn off the heat and remove the top of the double boiler. Let the butter cool for thirty minutes.

3. Line a strainer with 10 layers of cheesecloth. Place the strainer over a medium bowl, then pour the butter through the cheesecloth to catch the cannabis particles. Transfer the butter from the bowl to small tubs.

makes 1 pound

Blooming Flour

The use of cannabis in baking has a long and dubious tradition, at least where medical marijuana is concerned. That's because of the problems associated with determining dosages, as discussed earlier. Because baking is the most complex form of kitchen chemistry, bakers have perfected the techniques of blending various types of flours to create treats that would fail to bake properly if only one type of flour was used. Baking with blooming flour is much simpler. In the first place, we're not extracting—we're merely mixing and diluting so that the THC in the finished treat is measured and controlled. You will have to suffer through a few testings, but hey, it's all for the medicine.

When you're done baking, eat one of the baked items, like one cookie, wait until you feel buzzed or stoned, and judge the result. That will tell you a number of things about your reaction to the dosage: Is the cookie strong enough? If you felt nothing, obviously you should add more trim to the recipe. If one cookie did not relieve any symptoms, you can safely eat another. If two cookies relieved a symptom, that is a good dosage. I advise you to take notes on dosage levels for future baking with the trim from your marijuana garden.

1 ounce dried low-THC trim (any variety)

1. Pulverize the trim in a spice mill. Store it in a small screw-top jar, filling it almost to the top. Label the jar and keep it in the refrigerator until just before baking. It will keep indefinitely.

2. Add a measured amount of the trim to the flour in the recipe to be used in the baking— say $1/4$ cup trim to 1 cup flour, which I found to be a standard ratio. You may have to add a little more liquid to the mix to adjust for that extra dry material. That liquid could possibly be some melted Compounded Butter (page 134) or Cannoil (opposite), which would increase the THC level of the finished baked goods.

makes 1 ounce

Cannoil

Marijuana-infused vegetable, peanut, or olive oil can be used in most recipes that do not require high heat for cooking, and it is especially good in uncooked salad dressings. Since you're using so little oil in the dressing, a slight change of plan is necessary. If your goal is to consume the oil as part of, say, an infused olive oil and vinegar dressing, your oil will have to be more potent or you'll also need to consume other marijuana-laced foods. So consider infusing the olive oil with your higher-grade "bud leaves" or even—the horror!—some of your tops. Olive oil is great for infusing with

THC because you can dip breads and crackers into it and easily adjust both your dosage and your munchie cravings. To make a cooking oil, use peanut oil. Uses for cooking with cannoil include lower-heat baking and sautéing. Do not use cannoil of any type (vegetable, peanut, or olive) to deep-fry foods, because the temperature needed for deep-frying (375°F) is too hot for the THC. In particular, infused olive oil will smoke and deteriorate before that temperature is even reached.

1 ounce dried trim
2 cups vegetable, peanut, or olive oil

1. Pulverize the trim in a spice mill.

2. Heat the oil in a slow cooker on low. When the oil is hot, add the pulverized trim. Let the trim steep for 20 minutes, then let cool. Line a strainer with 10 layers of cheesecloth. Place the strainer over a medium bowl and pour the oil through the cheesecloth to catch the cannabis particles. Pour the oil into a jar, seal with a lid, and store in the refrigerator, where it will keep indefinitely.

makes 2 cups

Tincture of Cannabis

A *tincture* is simply an herb steeped in alcohol. If you don't like to smoke but don't mind drinking alcoholic beverages, this makes an excellent THC dispersal system. However, you will have to—don't be shocked—do a lot of testing and experimentation to determine your proper dosage. You can use trim or tops for this method, but tops are considered superior because they produce less of the weedy flavor of the trim. There is no need to crush the tops or blend the mixture—the vodka will efficiently extract the THC without help. You can also extract the THC with grain alcohol, which is 190 proof, but if you do, cut the amount of tincture by at least half for the following beverage recipes.

¼ ounce cured tops
1 liter vodka

1. In a large Mason jar, combine the tops and vodka. Place in a dark cabinet for a week, shaking the mixture once a day. When the tops have steeped for a week, strain the mixture through a coffee filter into another jar. Label and date the jar and place it in the refrigerator, where it will keep indefinitely.

Note: You will have to experiment to determine your dosage, but one writer on a cannabis forum states that he mixes 1 tablespoon of the tincture with a little fruit juice and "slugs it back." That is all he needs for about 3 hours of treatment, with the caveat that, like eating it, the effects take anywhere from 15 to 45 minutes to appear. Of course, you can use it as needed in any vodka mixed drink, but use caution or you could be doubly stoned.

makes about 3 cups

Beverages

Other than smoking, beverages are one of the easiest and fastest marijuana delivery systems. Please note that additional alcohol is a personal option in these recipes.

Double Mary Bloody Mary

Of course, part of your healing must involve multiple Marys. There are two ingredients in this recipe that are of paramount importance: the vodka tincture and a great habanero hot sauce. Considering all the options available for the latter, imbibers should have no problem selecting a commercial sauce. Note: I like my Bloody Marys shaken, not stirred!

2 teaspoons fresh lime juice, preferably Key limes
⅔ cup tomato juice or V-8
⅓ cup Tincture of Cannabis (page 137)
2 drops Worcestershire sauce
½ teaspoon habanero hot sauce
Freshly ground pepper
1 stalk celery with leaves or 1 green onion, sliced, for garnish

1. Fill a large mixing glass with ice cubes. Add the lime juice, tomato juice, Tincture of Cannabis, and Worcestershire. Add the habanero hot sauce, plus more to taste. Grind some pepper to taste into the drink.

2. Place a shaker on top of the mixing glass and, grasping them firmly together with both hands, shake vigorously 17 times. Remove the shaker, place a strainer on top of the mixing glass and strain the drink into a serving glass. Garnish with the celery or green onion.

serves 1

MJ Michelada—Spicy and Spacey Beer Cocktail

Michelada is a popular cocktail south of the border that has recently traveled north. It's a drink most Americans aren't familiar with unless they've traveled in Mexico or live in the border states. Essentially, it's a cocktail prepared with beer and hot sauce that's served over ice, and is very refreshing in the tropical heat. It has been touted as a surefire cure for hangovers, especially when the Tincture of Cannabis is added to it.

1 fresh lime, preferably Key lime
Coarse salt or margarita salt
2 dashes of Worcestershire sauce
1 dash of soy sauce
1 dash of habanero hot sauce
Freshly ground pepper

1 (12-ounce) bottle dark Mexican beer,
   such as Negra Modelo or Bohemia
⅓ cup Tincture of Cannabis (page 137)

1. Cut the lime in half. Rub one half around the rim of a large glass and reserve the other half. Pour the salt onto a plate and dip the rim of the glass in the salt to coat.

2. Fill the glass with ice and squeeze the juice from the reserved lime into the glass. Add the Worcestershire, soy, and habanero sauce along with a few grindings of pepper. Pour in the beer and Tincture of Cannabis, stir, and serve.

serves 1

12 ounces prepared hot chocolate (not too sweet)
2 tablespoons honey
1/2 teaspoon vanilla extract
1/3 cup Tincture of Cannabis (page 137)
2 tablespoons heavy cream
Cayenne pepper, for garnish

1. In a small pitcher, stir together the hot chocolate, honey, vanilla, and Tincture of Cannabis.

2. To serve, pour into cups and top with a drizzle of cream and a pinch of cayenne.

serves 2

Montezuma's Real Revenge

One of the culinary treasures that Cortez found when he invaded the Aztec empire of Mexico was the combination of chocolate and chile. Chiles and cacao pods were paid as tributes or taxes to the Emperor Montezuma, who was quite fond of the combination of the two. The Aztecs didn't have Old World marijuana, but they indulged in other drugs, namely peyote and tobacco. My friend Richard Sterling developed this recipe (without the tincture), which is his version of how the Spaniards transformed Montezuma's favorite beverage— with the addition of alcohol.

Salty Snacks

If you're not smoking marijuana, these recipes for munchies can ease your cravings before they begin. Remember, however, that snacks can be fattening.

1. In a large saucepan with a lid, heat the oil on medium-high heat. Place three-quarters of the popcorn in the oil and cover the saucepan. Shake the saucepan as the kernels begin popping. When most of the kernels have popped, remove the popcorn to a large serving bowl using a slotted spoon. Leave any unpopped kernels and excess oil in the saucepan.

2. Add the remaining kernels to the pan in an even layer. Cover the pan and shake it gently while the remaining kernels pop. When the popping slows down to 3 to 4 seconds between pops, remove the pan from the burner and transfer the popcorn to the serving bowl. Add the melted butter, plus more to taste, toss well, and serve.

makes 12 cups

Medicinal Popcorn

When the movie *Reefer Madness* played at the Biograph Theater in Richmond, Virginia, where I lived and worked in the early 1970s, it sold out Saturday nights at midnight for seventeen consecutive weeks—three different times! I can vouch for the fact that 90 percent of the moviegoers had adjusted attitudes when they arrived at the theater. Too bad the popcorn at the Biograph was bland.

¼ cup Cannoil (page 136) or vegetable oil
½ cup popcorn kernels
¼ cup Compounded Butter (page 134)

Spiced-Up and Powerful Pumpkin Seeds

Called *pepitas* in the Southwest, these baked pumpkin seeds are a very popular snack, especially when served with beer. You can substitute squash or sunflower seeds for the pumpkin seeds.

2 cups raw pumpkin seeds, hulled
⅓ teaspoon freshly ground pepper
1 teaspoon ground New Mexico red chile powder
½ teaspoon cumin
½ teaspoon salt

> continued

> *Spiced-Up and Powerful Pumpkin Seeds, continued*

Spicy, Sweet, Smoky, and Potent Peanuts

This interesting combination of flavors and sensations assumes that you like peanuts. If not, just about any small, real nut (the peanut is a legume, not a nut) can be substituted, but all of them are more expensive than peanuts.

2 cups unsalted, roasted peanuts
1 tablespoon Cannoil (page 136)
1 tablespoon sugar
$1/2$ tablespoon chipotle chile powder
1 teaspoon ground New Mexico red chile powder
Salt

1 tablespoon lime juice
$4^1/2$ tablespoons melted Compounded Butter (page 134)

1. Preheat the oven to 350°F and line a baking sheet with aluminum foil.

2. In a medium bowl, mix together the pumpkin seeds, pepper, chile powder, cumin, and salt. Add the lime juice and stir well. Spread the mixture evenly on the lined baking sheet and bake until golden brown, about 10 minutes. Remove the baking sheet from the oven and allow the seeds to cool before serving.

makes 2 cups

1. Preheat the oven to 250°F and line a baking sheet with aluminum foil.

2. In a large bowl, toss together the peanuts, Cannoil, sugar, and chile powders, making sure that the nuts are coated evenly. Arrange the nuts in a single layer on the baking sheet and bake for 30 minutes, stirring every 5 minutes. Remove the nuts from the oven, sprinkle with salt, and allow them to cool before serving.

makes 2 cups

Oven-Baked—I Mean, Like, Totally Baked—Potato Chips

Everyone has their food sins—those horrible things you eat when you know you shouldn't. My weakness is not chocolate, or Big Macs, or ice cream—it's potato chips. As with beer, I have to ration myself to avoid gaining weight. But getting baked with these chips might forgive the food sin!

3 tablespoons melted Compounded Butter
  (page 134)
1 tablespoon minced onion
1 teaspoon dried thyme
1½ teaspoons salt
4 medium potatoes, peeled and sliced very
  thinly using a mandoline

1. Preheat the oven to 350°F and grease a 9 by 13-inch pan.

2. In a small bowl, combine the butter, onion, thyme, and salt. Arrange the potatoes in the pan and brush them with butter mixture. Bake for 1 hour or until potatoes are crisp and beginning to brown. Periodically check on them so they don't burn. Store any leftovers in an airtight container.

serves 4

1. Preheat the oven to 350°F. In a small bowl, sift together the salt and the two flours. In a medium bowl, cream the butter by hand or using an electric hand mixer. Gradually add the cheese and the flour mixture to the butter.

2. Turn the dough onto a floured surface. Knead thoroughly. Divide dough into 2 pieces and, using a rolling pin, flatten each piece until it's about 1/8 inch thick. With a knife, cut the dough into straws about 6 inches long and gently twist them with your fingers. Arrange the straws on an ungreased cookie sheet and bake for 10 to 15 minutes, until golden. Remove the straws from the oven and transfer to a rack to cool. Store any leftovers in an airtight container.

makes 2 dozen

The Last Straw, and It's Cheesy

Ah, the classic snack cheese straws—the old Southern cocktail party treats. They originated in the days before adequate refrigeration as a way to preserve cheese, or at least its flavor, in a snack that would keep well in the cupboard. They became wildly popular because of this— and the fact that they are an excellent accompaniment to mixed drinks. But those Southern cooks never had any straws like these!

  1/2 teaspoon salt
  2 cups all-purpose flour
  1/4 cup Blooming Flour (page 135)
  1/2 cup Compounded Butter (page 134), softened
  1 pound Cheddar cheese, grated
  1/4 teaspoon cayenne, or more to taste

Parmesan Pita Crisps with Cannoil

Compared to the rest of the recipes in this chapter, these crisps are very low in healing power. But they are tasty, so you can eat a lot of them.

  6 (6-inch) pita flat breads
  1/4 cup Cannoil (page 136)
  1 1/2 cups finely grated imported Parmesan cheese
  Salt and freshly ground pepper

Scones, Muffins, and Cupcakes

Here are some easy-to-make baked treats. They are good for healing because they deliver the marijuana in discrete amounts that make it easy to adjust your dosage.

Sconed Again and Raisin Hell

Fortunately my wife, Mary Jane, knows how to make a mean scone. I've made her recipe even meaner with the addition of Blooming Flour and Compounded Butter.

1 large egg
½ cup milk
2 cups all-purpose flour
¼ cup Blooming Flour (page 135)
2½ tablespoons sugar
1 tablespoon baking powder
½ teaspoon salt
1 teaspoon lemon zest
6 tablespoons chilled Compounded Butter
   (page 134), plus more for serving
¾ cup raisins

1. Preheat the oven to 375°F. Cut each piece of bread into eight wedges. Arrange the wedges, with edges touching, on two ungreased baking sheets. With a pastry brush, spread oil on the top of each wedge. Sprinkle with Parmesan cheese and salt and pepper to taste.

2. On the middle and lower racks of the oven, bake the wedges for 12 to 15 minutes, until golden brown, switching the position of the sheets in the oven halfway through baking. Remove the crisps from the oven and place them on a rack to cool. Crisps may be made three days ahead and kept in an airtight container at room temperature.

serves 12

1. Preheat the oven to 350°F and line a baking sheet with aluminum foil. In a small bowl, whisk the egg and milk together. In a medium bowl, combine the two flours, sugar, baking powder, salt, and lemon zest. Using a pastry blender, cut the butter into the flour mixture

until the dough is pebbly. Add the egg mixture and mix with a fork until the dough is evenly moist. Add the raisins and stir until well mixed.

2. Spoon a dozen small mounds of dough onto the baking sheet and bake for 25 to 30 minutes, until the scones are golden brown. Serve warm topped with a little Compounded Butter.

makes 12

Lemon, Blueberry, and Double Ganja Muffins

Here's another double whammy of THC from the Blooming Flour and Compounded Butter. Because these muffins taste so good, you may be tempted to eat too many. Moderation, please—this is a dosage, not a competitive eating contest.

1³/₄ cups all-purpose flour
¹/₃ cup Blooming Flour (page 135)
1 tablespoon baking powder
¹/₂ teaspoon salt
1 large egg
1 cup sugar
¹/₄ cup Compounded Butter (page 134), melted
1¹/₃ cups sour cream
1¹/₂ cups frozen or fresh blueberries
1 tablespoon lemon zest

1. Preheat the oven to 350°F and line a muffin pan with 12 paper liners.

2. In a medium bowl, combine the two flours, baking powder, and salt; set aside. In a separate medium bowl, whisk the egg until light and fluffy, about 25 seconds. Add the sugar and whisk vigorously until thick, about 30 seconds. Add the melted butter in two or three portions, whisking to combine after each addition. Add the sour cream in two portions, whisking until just combined. Add the berries and lemon zest to the dry ingredients and gently toss until just combined. Using a spatula, fold the sour cream mixture into the dry mixture until the batter comes together and the berries are evenly distributed, 25 to 30 seconds. Small spots of flour may remain and the batter will be very thick. Do not overmix.

3. Using a large spoon or a cookie scoop sprayed with nonstick cooking spray, divide the batter among the prepared muffin cups. Bake for 25 to 30 minutes, until the muffins are light golden brown and a toothpick or thin knife inserted into the center of a muffin comes out clean. Immediately remove the muffins to a wire rack and let cool for at least 10 minutes. Serve warm or at room temperature.

makes 12

Energized Lemon–Poppy Seed Muffins

Need I remind you that poppy seeds have been known to trigger a positive response during drug tests? But we're not going to worry about that, are we? You will need to use a 16-cup muffin pan for this recipe or bake the muffins in batches.

1 cup Compounded Butter (page 134)
1 cup sugar
4 large eggs, separated
2 cups all-purpose flour
¼ cup Blooming Flour (page 135)
2 teaspoons baking powder
1 teaspoon salt
½ cup fresh lemon juice
2 tablespoons poppy seeds
3 teaspoons lemon zest

> continued

> *Energized Lemon–Poppy Seed Muffins, continued*

1. Preheat the oven to 350°F and line a muffin pan with 16 paper liners. Using an electric handheld mixer on high speed, cream together the butter and sugar in a large bowl until smooth. Add the egg yolks and beat until light and fluffy. In a separate bowl, sift the two flours, baking powder, and salt together. Add the dry ingredients alternately with lemon juice to the creamed mixture. Stir after each addition, but do not overmix.

2. In a medium bowl, beat egg whites until stiff. Fold the egg whites, poppy seeds, and lemon zest into the batter.

3. Divide the batter among the prepared muffin cups and bake for 25 minutes. Transfer the muffins to a wire rack and let cool for at least 10 minutes. Serve immediately or at room temperature.

makes 16

Carrot Cupcakes with Compounded Butter–Walnut Icing

This is probably over-the-top for a medical marijuana recipe, but hey, it's a very special treat. The frosting has nearly as much THC as the cupcakes themselves! Use a 12-cup muffin pan for this recipe.

⅓ cup softened Compounded Butter (page 134)
¼ cup brown sugar
½ cup sugar
1 tablespoon honey
1 tablespoon finely grated orange zest
2 large eggs
1 cup grated carrot
1 cup plus 2 tablespoons all-purpose flour
¼ cup Blooming Flour (page 135)
2 teaspoons baking powder
1 teaspoon ground cinnamon
¼ teaspoon ground allspice
½ teaspoon ground nutmeg
7 tablespoons freshly squeezed orange juice, warmed
1 teaspoon baking soda
½ cup chopped walnuts
¼ cup raisins

Compounded Butter–Walnut Icing
1 (8-ounce) package cream cheese, softened
1 teaspoon vanilla extract
½ cup softened Compounded Butter (page 134)
4 cups confectioners' sugar
1 cup chopped walnuts

1. Preheat the oven to 350°F and line a muffin pan with 12 paper liners. Using a handheld electric mixer on high speed, beat together the butter, two sugars, honey, and orange zest in a large bowl until pale and creamy. Beat in the eggs one at a time and then stir in the grated carrot.

2. In a medium bowl, sift together the flours, baking powder, cinnamon, allspice, and nutmeg. In a small bowl, stir together the orange juice and baking soda. Stir the flour mixture into the butter mixture in two portions, alternating with the orange juice mixture. With a spoon, stir in the walnuts and raisins until smooth. Do not overstir or the cupcakes will be tough.

3. Divide the batter among the prepared muffin cups. Bake for 20 minutes, until the cupcakes have risen and are lightly golden. Transfer the pan to a wire rack and let the cupcakes cool in the pan for 10 minutes, then turn them out onto a baking sheet and let them cool completely, about 1 hour.

4. To make the icing, using an electric mixer on low speed, beat the cream cheese, vanilla, and butter in a medium bowl until well combined. Slowly add the confectioners' sugar. Continue beating the mixture until smooth. Stir in the walnuts.

5. Frost the cooled cupcakes with the icing. The cupcakes can be stored in an airtight container for up to three days.

makes 12

Supercharged Chocolate Chip Cupcakes with Chocolate Frosting

This is for the chocoholics in the crowd. Use the best chocolate you can find with no sugar or milk in it. I'm not a big lover of sweets, but I can't resist a chocolate chip cookie of any kind, and I'm the same with these cupcakes.

1 cup all-purpose flour
1/8 cup Blooming Flour (page 135)
1 1/2 teaspoons baking powder
1/8 teaspoon salt
5 tablespoons softened Compounded Butter (page 134)
1/2 cup sugar
1 large egg
1/2 teaspoon vanilla extract
1/2 cup whole milk
1/2 cup dark chocolate chips

Chocolate Frosting
1/4 cup heavy cream
3/4 cup dark chocolate chips

> continued

> Supercharged Chocolate Chip Cupcakes, continued

1. Preheat the oven to 350°F and line a muffin pan with 12 paper liners. In a medium bowl, mix together the two flours, baking powder, and salt. Set aside.

2. Using a handheld electric mixer on high speed, beat together the butter and sugar in a large bowl until light and fluffy, then beat in the egg and the vanilla. With the mixer on low speed, add the flour mixture to the butter mixture in two portions, alternating with the milk. Fold in the chocolate chips and divide the batter among the lined muffin cups.

3. Bake on a rack set in the middle of the oven for 20 to 25 minutes or until a tester comes out clean. Transfer the cupcakes to a wire rack to cool completely.

4. To make the frosting, bring the cream to a simmer in a small heavy saucepan and add the chocolate chips, whisking until smooth. Let the frosting cool slightly to reach a spreadable consistency. Frost the cooled cupcakes with the icing. The cupcakes can be stored in an airtight container for up to three days.

makes 12

Cookies and Brownies

Here are some additional recipes for simple— yet delicious and effective—baked treats. I suggest eating a couple of these and waiting 30 minutes or so to see their effect before consuming any more of them.

Oatmeal-Raisin Cookies with Something Extra

I remember my mother making these (without the marijuana) almost on a daily basis during the holiday season, and my brother and I couldn't stop eating them. They're even better now.

½ cup all-purpose flour

⅛ cup Blooming Flour (page 135)

¼ teaspoon baking soda

¼ teaspoon salt

¼ teaspoon ground cinnamon

¼ teaspoon ground nutmeg

½ cup softened Compounded Butter (page 134)

¾ cup firmly packed brown sugar

1 large egg

½ teaspoon vanilla extract

1½ cups quick oats, uncooked

½ cup raisins

1. Preheat the oven to 375°F and line two baking sheets with parchment paper.

2. In a medium bowl, combine the flours, baking soda, salt, cinnamon, and nutmeg. Set aside.

3. In the large bowl of a stand mixer, cream the butter and sugar together for 2 to 3 minutes, until light and fluffy. Beat in the egg and vanilla. Gradually add the flour mixture and beat until well blended. Stir in the oats and raisins.

4. Drop rounded teaspoons of dough about 2 inches apart onto the parchment-lined baking sheets. Bake for 10 to 12 minutes, until golden brown. Transfer each sheet of parchment, keeping the cookies on it, to a wire rack to cool. Store cookies in an airtight container.

makes about 2 dozen

Mind-Boggling Chocolate Chip Cookies

Leo used Betty Crocker as his cookie dealer, but I'm going to be a bit more interesting here. The key is finding chocolate chips that are the darkest and finest available—at least 60 percent pure cacao. If you can't find the chips, buy a bar of the chocolate and dice it the same size as the chips. Yes, you will crack the bar and the "chips" won't be even, but who cares? This is medicine, right?

1½ cups Compounded Butter (page 134)

1¼ cups sugar

1¼ cups firmly packed brown sugar

1 tablespoon vanilla extract

2 large eggs

4 cups all-purpose flour

> continued

> *Mind-Boggling Chocolate Chip Cookies, continued*

½ cup Blooming Flour (page 135)
2 teaspoons baking soda
1 teaspoon salt
1 (24-ounce) package dark chocolate chips

1. Preheat the oven to 350°F.

2. In a large bowl using a wooden spoon, mix together the butter, sugars, vanilla, and eggs. Stir in the flours, baking soda, and salt. Then stir in the chocolate chips and mix well.

3. Drop rounded tablespoons of dough about 2 inches apart onto an ungreased cookie sheet. Bake for 12 to 15 minutes, until light brown. Transfer the cookies to a wire rack to cool. Store cookies in an airtight container.

makes about 5 dozen

1 teaspoon baking soda
¼ teaspoon salt
Green food coloring (optional)
Green sanding sugar (optional)

1. Preheat the oven to 350°F.

2. In a medium bowl, cream the butter by hand or using a handheld electric mixer on high speed and then beat in the sugar, egg, and extracts. In another bowl, sift together the dry ingredients and then add them to the butter mixture and mix well. Add enough food coloring to get the shade of green you like and mix well. Chill the dough in the refrigerator for 2 hours.

Not-Your-Usual Sugar Cookies

A company called Stonerware manufactures the cookie cutters essential to making this recipe (they're available from Amazon.com). I dare you to add the food coloring for an authentic color. Note that this recipe requires advance preparation.

½ cup Compounded Butter (page 134), softened
1 cup sugar
1 large egg
1 teaspoon vanilla extract
¼ teaspoon almond extract
1¾ cups cake flour, sifted
¼ cup Blooming Flour (page 135)

3. Using a rolling pin, roll out the dough on a floured surface until it is ⅛ inch thick. Use the marijuana leaf cookie cutter to cut out the cookies. Place them on ungreased cookie sheets and bake for about 7 minutes, until lightly browned. Remove from the oven, decorate with sanding sugar, and transfer to a rack to cool. Store cookies in an airtight container.

makes about 4 dozen

3. Using heaping teaspoonfuls of dough, shape into finger-like ovals and place on ungreased cookie sheets. Bake for 15 minutes, until lightly browned. Remove the sheets from the oven and place the cookies on racks to cool, at least 15 minutes.

4. Place confectioners' sugar in a shallow bowl. Roll the pecan fingers in the sugar to serve. (Now you are ready for your internal massage.) Store cookies in an airtight container.

makes 1 dozen

The Healing Touch of Pecan Fingers

These healing fingers work internally to relax, soothe, and inspire the imagination.

1 cup Compounded Butter (page 134)
$^1/_3$ cup confectioners' sugar, plus more for coating
$^1/_4$ teaspoon salt
1 teaspoon vanilla extract
1 tablespoon water
$1^3/_4$ cups all-purpose flour, sifted
$^1/_4$ cup Blooming Flour (page 135)
2 cups finely chopped pecans

1. Preheat the oven to 350°F.

2. In a medium bowl, cream the butter by hand or using a handheld electric mixer on high speed and then beat in $^1/_3$ cup of the sugar, the salt, vanilla, and water. Add the two flours and the pecans and mix well. Chill the dough for $^1/_2$ hour in the refrigerator.

The Return of the MJ Brownies

In the old days, we would stupidly add varying amounts of whatever cannabis we had lying around to a store-bought brownie mix and take our chances on how many brownies to eat. I remember—vaguely—going down some steps to a party after consuming just one. That is all I can remember of the party. This is the way to make MJ brownies correctly.

2 (4-ounce) bars semi-sweet chocolate
10 tablespoons softened Compounded Butter (page 134)
1 (8-ounce) package cream cheese, softened
2 cups sugar
6 large eggs
1 cup plus 2 tablespoons all-purpose flour
$1^1/_2$ teaspoons vanilla extract
1 teaspoon baking powder

> *continued*

½ teaspoon salt
2 tablespoons Blooming Flour (page 135)
1 cup finely chopped walnuts

1. Preheat the oven to 350°F and grease a 9 by 13-inch baking pan.

2. Using a double boiler, melt the chocolate and 6 tablespoons of the butter and then set aside to cool.

3. In a large bowl, cream the remaining 4 tablespoons of butter with the cream cheese by hand or using a handheld electric mixer on medium speed. To the butter and cream cheese mixture, add ½ cup of the sugar, 2 eggs, 2 tablespoons of the all-purpose flour, and 1 teaspoon of the vanilla and mix with a spatula until smooth. Set aside.

4. In a large mixing bowl and using an electric handheld mixer on medium speed, beat the remaining 4 eggs and 1½ cups of sugar. Add

the baking powder, salt, remaining 1 cup of all-purpose flour, and the Blooming Flour. Blend in the chocolate-butter mixture. Add in the remaining vanilla and the walnuts and mix thoroughly with a spatula.

5. Pour half of the chocolate mixture into the baking pan. Cover the chocolate mixture with the cream cheese mixture. Top with the remaining chocolate mixture. With a knife, zig-zag through the batter to create a marble effect.

6. Bake for 45 to 50 minutes, until a toothpick inserted in the center comes out clean. Remove the pan from the oven and set on a rack to cool for 30 minutes. Cover the pan with plastic or aluminum foil and store at room temperature for up to 5 days.

makes 24

Blasted Banana-Nut Bars

Bananas and nuts might indicate your condition after trying all of the recipes in this chapter on the same day, so please refrain from doing that—you'll gain too much weight!

1 cup cubed Compounded Butter (page 134)
½ cup water
1½ cups sugar
½ cup firmly packed brown sugar
1 cup mashed ripe bananas (about 2 medium)
½ cup buttermilk
2 large eggs

mixture, beating after each addition. Add the butter mixture and continue beating until well blended. Stir in the nuts and dates with a spatula and pour the batter into the prepared pan.

4. Bake for 18 to 22 minutes or until a toothpick inserted in the center comes out clean. Transfer the pan to a wire rack to cool. Cut into 2-inch-square bars and serve with calming milk.

makes about 30

1 teaspoon lemon zest

1 teaspoon vanilla extract

2 cups all-purpose flour

¼ cup Blooming Flour (page 135)

1 teaspoon baking soda

½ teaspoon grated nutmeg

½ cup chopped pecans or walnuts

½ cup pitted dates, chopped

1. Preheat the oven to 350°F and grease a 15 by 10 by 1-inch baking pan.

2. In a small saucepan, bring the butter and water to a boil. Remove from the heat and set aside.

3. In a large bowl and using a handheld electric mixer on medium speed, beat together the sugars, bananas, buttermilk, eggs, lemon zest, and vanilla until blended. In a separate bowl, combine the flours, baking soda, and nutmeg. Gradually add the flour mixture to the sugar

Candy

Here are the ultimate marijuana sweets, but you must embrace the concept of a healing candy. For people with a sweet tooth, this will be easy.

Toklas Revisited: Powerful Pecan Fudge

Everyone thinks that Alice B. Toklas (Gertrude Stein's companion) was making marijuana brownies, when in reality it was "Haschish [sic] Fudge." Here is the introduction to her recipe from *The Alice B. Toklas Cook Book* (1960): "This is the food of Paradise—of Baude-laire's Artificial Paradises: it might provide an entertaining refreshment for a Ladies' Bridge Club or a chapter meeting of the DAR. In Morocco it is thought to be good for ward-ing off the common cold in damp winter

1. Grease a 9 by 9-inch baking pan.

2. In a medium saucepan, mix together the sugar, milk, marshmallows, butter, and salt and cook over medium heat, stirring constantly until the mixture comes to a boil. Reduce the heat and cook for 5 minutes longer, stirring occasionally. Remove from the heat and stir in the pecans, chocolate chips, and vanilla.

3. Spread out smoothly in the prepared pan and refrigerate. When the fudge has cooled, cut it into small squares. Store it in an airtight container in the pantry for up to 5 days, or for up to 10 days in the refrigerator.

makes about 25

weather and is, indeed, more effective if taken with large quantities of hot mint tea. Euphoria and brilliant storms of laughter; ecstatic reveries and extensions of one's personality on several simultaneous planes are to be complacently expected."

That, of course, is in addition to the healing properties of this fudge, which is far less risky than the brownies I used to consume. Use the best chocolate chips you can find, or chop up a good dark chocolate bar.

    2 cups sugar
    ²/₃ cup evaporated milk
    12 large marshmallows
    ¹/₂ cup Compounded Butter (page 134)
    Pinch of salt
    1 cup finely chopped pecans
    1¹/₄ cups semisweet chocolate chips
    1 teaspoon vanilla extract

Almond–Compounded Butter Candy

An easy variant on pralines, this candy is so easy to make that even a medical-marijuana-impaired patient can make it.

    1 cup whole almonds
    ¹/₂ cup Compounded Butter (page 134)
    ¹/₂ cup sugar
    1 tablespoon light corn syrup

1. Grease a small baking sheet.

2. In a saucepan over medium heat, combine the almonds, butter, sugar, and corn syrup. Bring the mixture to a boil, stirring

constantly, and then boil for 5 minutes, stirring occasionally.

3. Spread the mixture on the prepared baking sheet and let cool until firm. With your hands or a mallet, break into pieces.

makes about 1½ cups

Picante Pirate Psychoactive Truffles

"Yo ho ho and a box of cannabis truffles" is the new pirate song these days, although the pirates of Somalia are still chewing khat or qat (*Catha edulis*). Don't go there, for cannabis is all the modern pirate needs to alleviate any pain resulting from his or her predations in the business world.

2 cups dark chocolate chips
⅓ cup Compounded Butter (page 134)
½ teaspoon habanero chile powder
¼ cup half and half
1 tablespoon rum
¼ cup minced fresh or rehydrated dried mango
Flaked or grated coconut, for garnish

1. In a microwave-safe bowl, combine the chocolate chips, butter, habanero powder, and half and half and microwave on 50 percent power for 1 minute. Remove, stir, and continue to cook on 50 percent power in 30-second increments until the chocolate is smooth and well blended. Stir in the rum and mango.

2. Refrigerate the mixture for about 15 minutes, until it is almost hard. Place the coconut in a bowl. Drop the candy by teaspoonfuls into the coconut. Shape the candies into 1-inch balls with your fingers.

makes about 3 dozen

Afterword

During my decades of researching chile peppers, one of the most commonly asked questions was, why did capsaicin evolve? Most scientists have speculated that the reason was to prevent mammals from eating the pods and destroying the seeds. This is a hypothesis based on observation. For hypotheses to become theories, they must be verified with substantial evidence and/or experimentation and generally accepted as true. A cohypothesis held that capsaicin is also a defense mechanism against microbial fungi that invade the pods through punctures made in the outer skin by various insects. But what if these hypotheses were not the real reason for capsaicin's evolution? Remember that chile peppers are the only known source of capsaicin.

Now consider cannabis, the only known source of THC. Traditional conjecture holds (as is the case with nicotine and caffeine) that the role of THC is to defend the marijuana plant from herbivores and pathogens. But if that's true, it doesn't do a very good job because a number of pests like whitefly, spider mites, thrips, and beetles attack it despite all those trichomes. And birds eat the seeds and thus spread marijuana, so why would a plant discourage this? Also remember that certain mammals eat the vegetative growth of marijuana, particularly deer and rodents.

Another hypothesis is that THC helps protect against ultraviolet radiation. There is more THC in plants found growing at high elevations where there is a greater concentration of UV rays. In my viewpoint, this suggests adaptation more than evolution, if, in fact, there is a cause-and-effect relationship. A final theory holds that THC reduces water loss. "Indeed, in very hot climates, the cuticle can split to allow the resin to ooze down the stems," writes Martin Booth in *Cannabis: A History*. "When caked on the plant, it hardens to an impermeable, water-insoluble varnish." Again, I think this is adaptation, not the real reason for the evolution of THC.

Humans have receptors that detect the presence of both capsaicin and THC and send those signals to the brain via the nervous system, blood circulation, or both. Whether it's a burning sensation or a high, it's the same process. And how did those receptors originate? I think from the coevolution of humankind with both chile peppers and marijuana.

Put simply, *coevolution* is the situation where two different species help each other adapt and reproduce by influencing each other. The coevolution of bees with flowers is probably the classic case, and that type of coalition is called *mutualistic coevolution* because both species receive a benefit as a result of it. The flowers get pollinated and the bees receive nectar and pollen. They both enhance the other's ability to survive and reproduce. It's my hypothesis that both capsaicin and THC evolved to encourage humans to domesticate these two plants and give them a much better chance to survive. After all, given the total number of seeds produced by a typical cannabis plant, I think it's pretty obvious that a higher percentage of seeds will thrive under human care rather than in the wild conditions of the foothills of the Indian Kush. But some people disagree. In one of his lectures in 2002, author and journalism professor Michael Pollan is quoted as saying, "Why did this plant make THC in the first place, THC being the main psychoactive ingredient? It certainly wasn't so people could get high. Marijuana did not produce THC so we could change our consciousness." Robert Connell Clarke, the author of *Marijuana Botany* (1981), disagrees and writes that "the most obvious evolutionary advantage THC conferred on cannabis was the psychoactive properties which attracted human attention and caused the plant to be spread around the world."

But in his book *The Botany of Desire* (2001), Pollan noted that the vast majority of botanists have what he calls a "blinkered humanist

A blast from the past: my crop in the grow barn

perspective." They simply ignore the coevolution of humans and cannabis. "We automatically think of domestication as something we do to other species," he explains, "but it makes just as much sense to think of it as something certain plants and animals have done to us, a clever evolutionary strategy for advancing their own interests . . . a dance of human and plant desire that has left neither the plants nor the people taking part in it unchanged."

What we humans have inherited are *endocannabinoids* and *endocapsaicinoids*, compounds within our bodies that are essentially identical to those found in marijuana and chile peppers. One researcher, Dr. Gregory T. Carter of the University of Washington, was quoted on CMT News Archives explaining some of the current knowledge of the cannabis-like compounds in our bodies: "It now appears that the cannabinoid system evolved with our species and is intricately involved in normal human physiology, specifically in the control of movement, pain, memory, and appetite, among others. The detection of widespread cannabinoid receptors in the brain and peripheral tissues suggests that the cannabinoid system represents a previously unrecognized ubiquitous network in the nervous system."

If you agree with Carter's hypothesis, then you also believe, as I do, that we are genetically preprogrammed to enjoy the high produced by cannabis and its medicinal properties as well as the burn resulting from chile peppers. In this marijuana grow guide, I've avoided taking a political stance, but my point in this afterword is that, in the past, attempts at regulating drug use through federal legislation have failed miserably. Prohibition and the fact that cancer-causing cigarettes are still legal are two examples of inconsistent and failed federal government thinking about the nature of drugs and human dependence upon them. At least a growing number of state legislatures have realized that the war on drugs declared by federal authorities can never be won and have legalized the personal consumption and cultivation of marijuana. Thus the growing techniques described in this book can be legally practiced in many of those states.

This was not the case when I was growing back in the early '70s, and readers of this book may be wondering whatever happened to the combination barn and greenhouse I illegally grew marijuana in. Well, I had a great crop but most of it got ripped off at gunpoint. Part of the stolen crop was recovered with no one hurt and no cops involved. That was the end of my second marijuana-growing career, and that debacle made me paranoid and very security conscious. Fortunately, the third and final marijuana growing career terminated peacefully when Mary Jane finally got fed up with the illegal plants, and I ditched them to keep peace in the family. A good thing, too—it happened before the state police and DEA agents arrived. That grow barn is now a well-lit horse barn.

Resources

While buying local and paying cash is preferable, it's not always possible. If you buy your supplies online, I recommend the sources listed here.

Benches, Light Racks, and Grow Stands

West Coast Growers
westcoastgrowers.com
A wide variety of indoor-growing apparatus, from lights and racks to fans and dehumidifiers.

Grow Rooms and Tents

BC Northern Lights
bcnorthernlights.com
Growing boxes and hydroponic equipment.

Dealzer
dealzer.com
Growing boxes, tents, and hydroponic equipment.

Horticultural Portable Grow Room
everestgardensupply.com
Grow lighting, grow rooms, and harvesting equipment.

Hydro Grow Rooms

hydrowholesale.com
Grow lights, accessories, and tents.

Monster Gardens

monstergardens.com
Grow rooms, controllers, lighting, and harvesting equipment.

Super Closet

supercloset.com
Automated grow rooms, closets, and trailers.

Harvesting Equipment

TrimPro

trimpro.com
Automatic trimming devices.

Trim Scene Solutions

trimscene.com
Drying racks, trimmers, scissors, and general harvesting equipment.

Lighting and Fans

Home Grow Depot

homegrowdepot.com
A wide variety of marijuana growing equipment.

DH Warehouse & Superstore

discount-hydro.com
A good selection of discount hydroponic equipment.

HID Hut

hidhut.com
Specializing in grow light kits, but has a wide selection of indoor growing apparatus.

Phototron

growlifeinc.com
Manufacturer of Phototron indoor growing systems for a wide variety of plants.

Quantum Horticulture

quantumhort.com
Manufacturer of dimmable, electronic lighting ballasts.

SunPulse

sunpulselamps.com
Manufacturer of digital HID lamps.

Lighting Controllers

Power Box
powerboxinc.com
Many types of lighting controllers.

Marijuana Consumption Apparatus

Aqua Lab Technologies
aqualabtechnologies.com
Glassware, pipes, and vaporizers.

Everyone Does It
everyonedoesit.com
Bongs, pipes, grinders, storage containers, papers, and accessories.

Pest Control

Hemp Diseases and Pests: Management and Biological Control, by J. M. McPartland, R. C. Clarke, and D. P. Watson (CABI, 2000). A recommended book; I hope that you never have to consult it.

Security Equipment

These two companies are not specifically devoted to marijuana-growing security, but they specialize in general home and business security.

Dakota Alert Co.
dakotaalert.com
Wireless security equipment.

Northern Tool & Equipment Co.
www.northerntool.com/shop/tools/category_security-equipment
Motion detectors, alarms, and cameras.

Seed Sources

These companies cooperated with Leo and me in the writing of this book. For the latest seed company ratings, see seedbankupdate.com.

Attitude Bank
cannabis-seeds-bank.co.uk

Barney's Farm
barneysfarm.com

Bonguru Beans
bonguruseeds.com

Dinafem Seeds
dinafem.org

Dr. Greenthumb
drgreenthumb.com

Green House Seed Co.
greenhouseseeds.nl
Note that residents of the United States and
Canada can't buy from their online store.

Mandala Seeds
mandalaseeds.com

Soma Seeds
somaseeds.nl

Soils and Fertilizers

Advanced Nutrients
advancednutrients.com
Growing gear and a wide selection
of fertilizers.

Scientific Soils
scientificsoils.com
Premium planting mixes.

Storage

420 Science
420science.com
Storage containers and optical devices.

CannaFresh
cannafresh.com
Display and storage products for the medical
marijuana industry.

TightPac
tightpac.com
Airtight, water-resistant, light-resistant
storage containers.

Waterers

Gardener's Supply Company
gardeners.com
Drip-It Waterers available, along with
soaker hoses.

Bibliography

Anonymous. "Cannabinoids in Cannabis." Canadian Consortium for the Investigation of Cannabis. Accessed July 17, 2011. http://wilstar.com/theories.htm.

———. "Scientific Laws, Hypotheses, and Theories." Accessed August 11, 2011. http://www.ccic.net/index.php?id=255,733,0,0,1,0.

———. "17 Legal Medical Marijuana States and DC: Laws, Fees, and Possession Limits." Accessed June 12, 2011. http://medicalmarijuana.procon.org/view.resource. php?resourceID=000881.

Biksa, Erik. "Optimize Your Growing Environment." *The Best of High Times: Grow Guide 2011* 61 (July 2011): 24–28.

Booth, Martin. *Cannabis: A History.* New York: St. Martin's Press, 2004.

Carter, Gregory. "Cannabis: Old Medicine with a New Promise." Revised 2002. http://www.lindacrabtree.com/cmt/drugs/drugs_article6.html.

Cervantes, Jorge. *Marijuana Horticulture: The Indoor/Outdoor Medical Grower's Bible.* Vancouver, WA: Van Patten Publishing, 2006.

Clarke, Robert Connell. *Marijuana Botany.* Berkeley, CA: Ronin Publishing, 1981.

Cooke, Mordecai Cubitt. *The Seven Sisters of Sleep: Popular History of the Seven Prevailing Narcotics of the World.* London: James Blackwood, 1860.

Drake, William Daniel, Jr. *The Connoisseur's Handbook of Marijuana.* New York: Simon & Schuster, 1971.

———. *The International Cultivator's Handbook.* Berkeley, CA: Wingbow Press, 1974.

Elsohly, Mahmoud A. "Quarterly Report #104, University of Mississippi Potency Monitoring Project." Oxford, MS: National Center for Natural Products Research, a division of the Research Institute of Pharmaceutical Sciences, 2008.

Fichter, George S. *Insect Pests.* New York: Golden Press, 1966.

Fuller, Harry J., and Donald D. Ritchie. *General Botany.* 5th ed. New York: Barnes & Noble, 1967.

Goldacre, Ben. "Reefer Badness." *The Guardian*, March 24, 2007.

Green, Greg. *The Cannabis Grow Bible.* 2nd ed. San Francisco: Green Candy Press, 2010.

Hager, Paul. "Marijuana Myths." *Cannabis Culture Magazine.* July 2011. http://www.drugtext.org/Cannabis-marijuana-hashisch/marijuana-myths.html.

Harrison, David. "The Buying and Selling of Legal Marijuana." Accessed September 29, 2010. http://www.pewstates.org/projects/stateline/headlines/the-buying-and-selling-of-legal-marijuana-85899376777.

High, Will B. *Weedopedia: A Totally Dank A–Z Reference.* Avon, MA: Adams Media, 2010.

Iverson, Leslie L. *The Science of Marijuana.* 2nd ed. New York: Oxford University Press, 2008.

Jiëder, Hugh, and Mike Utah. "Indoor Organic Pest Control, Part 2." *High Times* 416 (September 2010): 38.

Joint Doctor, "Official Lowryder Grow Guide, 2004." Accessed August 11, 2011. http://www.lowryderseeds.eu/lowryder-grow-guide.html.

Krukonis, Greg. *Evolution for Dummies*. Hoboken, NJ: Wiley Publishing, 2008.

Lee, Tina. "The Wick Method." *Cannabis Culture Magazine*. Revised August 15, 2001. http://www.cannabisculture.com/articles/2077.html.

Maass, Brian. "Mobile Medical Marijuana Trailer Stolen." Accessed April 6, 2011. http://denver.cbslocal.com/2011/04/06/mobile-medical-marijuana-trailer-stolen/.

Mathew, Litty. "Edible Weed." *Saveur*. (June–July 2011): 22.

McKenna, Terence. *Food of the Gods*. New York: Bantam Books, 1992.

Pollan, Michael. *The Botany of Desire*. New York: Random House, 2001.

———. "Cannabis, Forgetting, and the Botany of Desire." Berkeley, CA: Occasional Papers, Townsend Center for the Humanities, UC Berkeley, 2003. http://escholarship.org/uc/item/4000045b.

Rosenthal, Ed. *The Big Book of Buds 2*. Oakland, CA: Quick American, 2004.

———. *The Big Book of Buds 3*. Oakland, CA: Quick American, 2007.

Russo, Ethan B., et al. "Phytochemical and Genetic Analyses of Ancient Cannabis from Central Asia." *Journal of Experimental Botany* 59, no. 14, 2008: 4171–82.

Ruttle, Jack. "Rubbish." *National Gardening*. (May–June 1992): 38.

Schultes, Richard Evans. *Hallucinogenic Plants*. New York: Golden Press, 1976.

———, and W. M. Klein, T. Plowman, and T. E. Lockwood. "Cannabis: An Example of Taxonomic Neglect." Botanical Museum Leaflets, Harvard University 23, no. 9, 1974: 337–64.

Severson, Kim. "Marijuana Fuels a New Kitchen Culture." *New York Times*, nytimes.com, May 18, 2010. http://www.nytimes.com/2010/05/19/dining/19pot.html?_r=1&pagewanted=all.

Slayton, Joyce. "The French Laundry of the Weed World?" Accessed August 25, 2010. http://www.chow.com/food-news/57523/the-french-laundry-of-the-weed-world/.

Starks, Michael. *Marijuana Chemistry: Genetics, Processing and Potency*. 2nd ed. Berkeley, CA: Ronin Publishing, 1993.

Sumach, Alexander. *A Treasury of Hashish*. Toronto, Ontario: Stoneworks Publishing Co., 1976.

Toklas, Alice B. *The Alice B. Toklas Cook Book*. New York: Anchor Books, 1960.

Weil, Andrew. *The Natural Mind*. Boston: Houghton Mifflin Co., 1972.

———. *The Marriage of the Sun and Moon*. Boston: Houghton Mifflin Co., 1980.

Wercshop Blog; "incrEDIBLE Variability," blog entry by Anonymous, July 25, 2011. http://thewercshop.com/category/analysis/.

Acknowledgments

Special thanks to Leo Lascaux, essentially the coauthor-in-hiding of this book, for letting me invade his life for a few months. (He's also a very good editor.) For the others who helped produce it, an *abrazo grande* to all of you: My editor Julie Bennett, who transformed a rogue manuscript into the book she wanted; Marlin Bensinger, who helped with the chemistry; Lois Manno, who directed the photography; Emily DeWitt-Cisneros and Mary Jane Wilan, who collaborated on cooking the medical marijuana recipes in chapter 10; Giordano Bruno, who provided some nice indoor photos; Scott Mendel, my longtime agent who makes all these book projects happen; and Wes Naman, who lovingly photographed a favorite subject of his.

About the Author

Photo credit: Don James

A food historian and one of the foremost international experts on capsicums, Dave DeWitt has written or coauthored more than forty books, mostly on chile peppers and fiery foods, and has edited two magazines on the subjects. His other major horticultural interest is marijuana, specifically medical marijuana. He has been a radio announcer and television producer and has appeared on many national television programs.

Dave is chair of the board of the New Mexico Farm and Ranch Heritage Museum and an adjunct associate professor at New Mexico State University. He holds a bachelor's degree in English from the University of Virginia and a master's degree in English from the University of Richmond.

Sunbelt Shows, Inc., which Dave owns with his wife, Mary Jane Wilan, is a media company that specializes in fiery foods and barbecue. Sunbelt Shows has produced the annual National Fiery Foods and Barbecue Show since 1988.

Index